German Society at the Close of the Middle Ages by Ernest Belfort Bax
Prism Key Press | www.prismkeypress.com

ISBN: 978-1463637972

German Society at the Close of the Middle Ages

Ernest Belfort Bax

Contents

Preface

The work, of which the present volume is the first instalment, aims at giving English readers a general view of the social condition and the popular movements of Germany during the period known as that of the Reformation. In accordance with this plan, I have only touched incidentally upon the theological disputes then currently uppermost in the thoughts of men, or upon the purely political side of things. They are dealt with merely in so far as they immediately strike across the path of social and internal affairs. The present volume, which has a more general character than its successors, deals with a period limited, roughly speaking, by the closing years of the fifteenth century on the one side, and by 1525, the veer of the great Peasant rising on the other. It contains narrative of the earlier popular revolutionary movements at the close of the Middle Ages, the precursors of the Peasants' War; and it also deals with the underlying causes, economic, social and juridical, of the general disintegration of the time.

The next volume will treat more in detail the events of the rears 1524 to 1526. The third will contain a history of the Anabaptist Movement in Central Europe from its rise at Zwickau in 1522 to its decline after the capture of Münster by the Archiepiscopal and Imperial troops in 1536. The reign of the Saints in Münster naturally forms the leading feature of this portion of the work.

As to the sources for the history of the Germany of this period, I have endeavoured to incorporate everything available that seemed to me important for the proper understanding of the time. The three chief general histories of the Reformation, Ranke's *Geschichte Deutschlands während der Reformations-Zeit,* Janssen's *Geschichte des Deutschen Volkes,* and Egelhaafs *Deutsche Geschichte im sechszehnten Jahrhundert,* have, it is scarcely necessary to say, been laid under contribution. The standpoint of Ranke, whose history is detailed and in certain respects exhaustive, is that of general bourgeois Philistinism. Janssen represents the Ultramontane Catholic view; but, apart from its tendency, every one must admire the brilliant and in most cases accurate scholarship that characterises it. Egelhaaf's work may be regarded as the counterblast to Janssen's. Its point of view is that of "liberal," middle-class German Protestantism; but it also contains many hints and clues which may be followed up by the industrious historian.

To rewrite history in the light of the researches of the later decades of the nineteenth century will be the great task of the next two or three generations. History has to be presented afresh on the basis of primitive communism with its tribal and village groups, with its sexual relations based on the *gens*, with its totemistic religious conceptions, and from the standpoint of a continuous development from these beginnings up to the individualism of the present day founded on the complete disruption of early society.

The average student of any historical period invariably reads into his interpretation the intellectual, moral and social atmosphere that lies nearest to him. He cannot strip away the intervening time-content between himself and the period in question. It is the most difficult of all exercises of the imagination, and to most men, indeed, impossible, to realise that the same words, names, customs and institutions connote totally different actualities in different stages of historic evolution. People fail to conjure up the altered perspective, and the unfamiliar background on which men lived, thought and felt in another age. Agamemnon, "king of Men," is to them Kaiser Wilhelm differently made up. Lykurgos is a cross between Pitt and Dr. Johnson. Cicero is a Sir Charles Russell who happened to live in the first century B.C. The formal continuity of names, notions or things hides from them the "true inwardness" of the rupture between the old and the new which has gradually accomplished itself. Change in human affairs is of course ceaseless ; but it is only when it has reached a certain stage that it is borne in upon the consciousness of men in general, and, even then, it is only the sharp summits above the changing horizon that they recognise. The ground out of which these spring is not seen, and hence the true bearing of the summits themselves is not understood.

Introduction

The close of the fifteenth century had left the whole structure of mediaeval Europe to all appearance intact. Statesmen and writers like Philip de Commines had apparently as little suspicion that the state of things they saw around them, in which their had grown up and of which they were representatives, was ever destined to pass away, as Lord Palmerston or any other statesman of the Cobden-Bright period had that the existing system of society, say in 1860, was at any time likely to suffer other changes than those of detail. Society was organised on the feudal hierarchy of status. In the first place, a noble class, spiritual and temporal, was opposed to a peasantry either wholly servile or but nominally free. In addition to this opposition of noble and peasant there was that of the township, which, in its corporate capacity, stood in the relation of lord to the surrounding peasantry.

The township in Germany was of two kinds — first of all, there was the township that was "free of the Empire," that is, that nominally from the Emperor himself (*Reichstadt*), and secondly, there was the township that was under the domination of an intermediate lord. The economic basis of the whole was still land; the status of a man or of a corporation was determined by the mode in which they held their land. "No land without a lord" was the principle of mediaval polity; just as "money has no master" is the basis of the bourgeois world with its self-made men. Every distinction of rank in the feudal system was still denoted for the most part by a special costume. It was a world of knights in armour, of ecclesiastics in vestments and stoles, of lawyers in robes, of princes in silk and velvet and cloth of gold, and of peasants in laced shoe, brown cloak, and cloth hat.

But although the whole feudal organisation was outwardly intact, the thinker who was watching the signs of the times would not have been long in arriving at the conclusion that feudalism was "played out," that the whole fabric of mediaeval civilisation was becoming dry and withered, and had either already begun to disintegrate or was on the eve of doing so. Causes of change had within the past half-century been working underneath the surface of social life, and were rapidly undermining the whole structure. The growing use of fire-arms in war; the rapid multiplication of printed books; the spread of the new learning after the taking of Constantinople in 1453, and the subsequent diffusion of Greek teachers throughout Europe; the surely and steadily increasing communication with the new world, and the consequent increase of the precious metals; and, last but not least, Vasco de Gama's discovery of the new trade route from the East by way of the Cape — all these were indications of the fact that the death-knell of the old order of things had been struck.

Notwithstanding the apparent outward integrity of the system based on land tenures, land was ceasing to be the only form of productive wealth. Hence it was losing the exclusive importance attaching to it in the earlier period of the Middle Ages. The first form of modern capitalism had already arisen. Large aggregations of capital in the hands of trading companies were becoming common. The Roman law was establishing itself in the place of the old customary tribal law which had hitherto prevailed in the manorial courts, serving in some sort as a bulwark against the caprice of the territorial lord; and this change facilitated the development of the bourgeois principle of private, as opposed to communal, property. In intellectual matters, though theology still maintained its supremacy as the chief subject of human interest, other interests were rapidly growing up alongside of it, the most prominent being the study of classical literature.

Besides these things, there was the dawning interest in nature, which took on, as a matter of course, a magical form in accordance with traditional and contemporary modes of thought. In fact, like the flicker of a dying candle in its socket, the Middle Ages seemed at the beginning of the sixteenth century to exhibit all their own salient characteristics in an exaggerated and distorted form. The old feudal relations had degenerated into a blood-sucking oppression; the old rough brutality, into excogitated and elaborated cruelty (aptly illustrated in the collection of ingenious instruments preserved in the Torture-tower at Nürnberg); the old crude superstition, into a systematised magical theory of natural causes and effects; the old love of pageantry, into a lavish luxury and magnificence of which we have in the "field of the cloth of gold" the stock historical example; the old chivalry, into the mercenary bravery of the soldier, whose trade it was to tight, and who recognised only one virtue — to wit, animal courage. Again, all these exaggerated characteristics were mixed with new elements, which distorted them further, and which foreshadowed a coming change, the ultimate issue of which would be their extinction and that of the life of which they were the signs.

The growing- tendency towards centralisation and the consequent suppression or curtailment of the local autonomies of the Middle Ages in the interests of some kind of national government, of which the political careers of Louis XI. in France, of Edward IV. in England, and of Ferdinand and Isabella in Spain were such conspicuous instances, did not fail to affect in a lesser degree that loosely connected political system of German States known as the Holy Roman Empire. Maximilian's first Reichstag in 1495 caused to be issued an imperial edict suppressing the right of private warfare claimed and exercised by the whole noble class from the princes of the Empire down to the meanest knight. In the same year the Imperial Chamber (*Reichskammer*) was established, and in 1501 the Imperial Aulic Council. Maximilian also organised a standing army of mercenary troops, called *Landesknechte.* Shortly afterwards Germany was divided into imperial districts called circles (*Kreise*), ultimately ten in number, all of which were under a *Reichsregiment,* which had at its disposal a military force for the punishment of disturbers of the peace. But the public opinion of the age, conjoined with the particular circumstances, political and economic, of central

Europe, robbed the enactment in a great measure of its immediate effect. Highway plundering and even private war was still going on, to a considerable extent, far into the sixteenth century. Charles V. pursued the same line of policy; but it was not until after the suppression of the lower nobility in 1523, and finally of the peasants in 1526, that any material change took place; and then the centralisation, such as it was, was in favour of the princes, rather than of the imperial power, which, after Charles V.'s time, grew weaker and weaker. The speciality about the history of Germany is, that it has not known till our own day centralisation on a national or racial scale like England or France.

At the opening of the sixteenth century public opinion not merely sanctioned open plunder by the wearer of spurs and by the possessor of a stronghold, but regarded it as his special prerogative, the exercise of which was honourable rather than disgraceful. The cities certainly resented their burghers being waylaid and robbed, and hanged the knights whenever they could; and something like a perpetual feud always existed between the wealthier cities and the knights who infested the trade routes leading to and from them. Still, these belligerent relations were taken as a matter of course; and no disgrace, in the modern sense, attached to the occupation of highway robbery.

In consequence of the impoverishment of the knights at this period, owing to causes with which we shall deal later, the trade or profession had recently received an accession of vigour, and at the same time was carried on more brutally and mercilessly than ever before. We will give some instances of the sort of occurrence which was by no means unusual. In the immediate neighbourhood of Nürnberg, which was *bien entendu* one of the chief seats of the imperial power, a robber-knight leader, named Hans Thomas von Absberg, was a standing menace. It was the custom of this ruffian, who had a large following, to plunder even the poorest who came from the city, and, not content with this, to mutilate his victims. In June, 1522, he fell upon a wretched craftsman, and with his own sword hacked off the poor fellow's right hand, notwithstanding that the man begged him upon his knees to take the left, and not destroy his means of earning his livelihood. The following August he, with his band, attacked a Nürnberg tanner, whose hand was similarly treated, one of his associates remarking that he was glad to set to work again, as it was "a long time since they had done any business in hands ". On the same occasion a cutler was dealt with after a similar fashion. The hands in these cases were, collected and sent to the bürgermeister of Nürnberg, with some such phrase as that the sender (Hans Thomas) would treat all so who came from the city. The princes themselves, when it suited their purpose, did not hesitate to offer an asylum to these knightly robbers. With Absberg were associated Georg von Giech and Hans George von Aufsess. Among other notable robber-knights of the time may be mentioned the Lord of Brandenstein and the Lord of Rosenberg. As illustrating the strictly professional character of the pursuit, and the brutally callous nature of the society practising it, we may narrate that Margaretha von Brandenstein was accustomed, it is recorded, to give the advice to the choice guests round her board that when a merchant failed to keep his promise to them, they should never hesitate to cut off *both* his hands. Even Franz yon Sichingen, known sometimes as the "last flower of German chivalry," boasted of having among the intimate associates of his enterprise for the rehabilitation of knighthood many gentlemen who had peen accustomed to "let their horses on the high road bite off the purses of wayfarers". So strong was the public opinion of the noble class as to the inviolability of the privilege of highway plunder that a monk, preaching one day in a cathedral and happening to attack it as unjustifiable, narrowly escaped death at the hands of some knights present amongst his congregation, who asserted that he had insulted the prerogatives of their order. Whenever this form of knight-errantry was criticised, there were never wanting scholarly pens to defend it as a legitimate means of aristocratic livelihood; since a knight must live in suitable style, and this was often his only resource for obtaining the means thereto.

The free cities, which were subject only to imperial jurisdiction, were practically independent republics. Their organisation was a microcosm of that of the entire Empire. At the apex of the municipal society was the Bürgermeister and the so-called "Honorability" (*Ehrbarkeit*), which consisted of the patrician *gentes*, (in most cases) those families which were supposed to be descended from the original chartered freemen of the town, the old Mark-brethren. They comprised generally the richest families, and had monopolised the entire government of the city, together with the right to administer its various sources of income and to consume its revenue at their pleasure. By the time, however, of which we are writing the trading guilds had also attained to a separate power of their own, and were in some cases ousting the burgher-aristocracy, though they were very generally susceptible of being manipulated by the members of the patrician class, who, as a rule, could alone sit in the Council (*Rath*). The latter body stood, in fact, as regards the town, much in the relation of the feudal lord to his manor. Strong in their wealth and in their aristocratic privileges, the patricians lorded it alike over the townspeople and over the neighbouring peasantry, who were subject to the municipality. They forestalled and regrated with impunity. They assumed the chief rights in the municipal lands, in many cases imposed duties at their own caprice, and turned guild privileges and rights of citizenship into a source of profit for themselves. Their bailiffs in the country districts forming part of their territory were often more voracious in their treatment of the peasants than even the nobles themselves. The accounts of income and expenditure were kept in the loosest manner, and embezzlement clumsily concealed was the rule rather than the exception.

The opposition of the non-privileged citizens, usually led by the wealthier guildsmen not belonging to the aristocratic class, operated through the guilds and through the open assembly of the citizens. It had already frequently succeeded in establishing a representation of the general body of the guildsmen in a so-called

Great Council (*Grosser Rath*), and in addition, as already said, in ousting the "honorables" from some of the public functions. Altogether the patrician party, though still powerful enough, was at the opening of the sixteenth century already on the decline, the wealthy and unprivileged opposition beginning in its turn to constitute itself into a quasi-aristocratic body as against the mass of the poorer citizens and those outside the pale of municipal rights. The latter class was now becoming an important and turbulent factor in the life of the larger cities. The craft-guilds, consisting of the body of non-patrician citizens, were naturally in general dominated by their most wealthy section.

We may here observe that the development of the mediaeval township from its earliest beginnings up to the period of its decay in the sixteenth century was almost uniformly as follows:[1] At first the township, or rather what later became the township, was represented entirely by the group *of gentes* or group — families originally settled within the mark or district on which the town subsequently stood. These constituted the original aristocracy from which the tradition of the *Ehrbarkeit* dated. In those towns founded by the Romans, such as Trier, Aachen, and others, the case was of course a little different. There the origin of the *Ehrbarkeit* may possibly be sought for in the leading families of the Roman provincials who were in occupation of the town at the coming of the barbarians in the fifth century. Round this nucleus there gradually accreted from the earliest period of the Middle Ages the freed men of the surrounding districts, fugitive serfs, and others who sought that protection and means of livelihood in a community under the immediate domination of a powerful lord, which they could not otherwise obtain when their native village-community had perchance been raided by some marauding noble and his retainers. Circumstances, amongst others the fact that the community to which they attached themselves had already adopted commerce and thus become a guild of merchants, led to the differentiation of industrial functions amongst the new-comers, and thus to the establishment of craft-guilds.

Another origin of the townsfolk, which must not be overlooked, is to be found in the attendants on the palace-fortress of some great overlord. In the early Middle Ages all such magnates kept up an extensive establishment, the greater, ecclesiastical lords no less than the secular often having several palaces. In Germany this origin of the township was furthered by Charles the Great, who established schools and other civil institutions, with a magistrate at their head, round many of the palaces that he founded. "A new epoch," says Von Maurer, "begins with the villa-foundations of Charles the Great and his ordinances respecting them, for that his celebrated capitularies in this connection were intended for his newly established villas is self-evident. In that proceeding he obviously had the Roman villa in his mind, and on the model of this he rather further developed the previously existing court and villa constitution than completely reorganised it. Hence one finds even in his new creations the old foundation again, albeit on a far more extended plan, the economical side of such villa-colonies being especially more completely and effectively ordered."[2] The expression "Palatine," as applied to certain districts, bears testimony to the fact here referred to. As above said, the development of the township was everywhere on the same lines. The aim of the civic community was always to remove as far as possible the power which controlled them. Their worst condition was when they were immediately overshadowed by a territorial magnate. When their immediate lord was a prince, the area of whose feudal jurisdiction was more extensive, his rule was less oppressively felt, and their condition was therefore considerably improved. It was only, however, when cities were "free of the Empire" (*Reichsfrei*) that they attained the ideal of mediaeval civic freedom.

It follows naturally from the conditions described that there was, in the first place, a conflict between the primitive inhabitants as embodied in their corporate society and the territorial lord, whoever he might be. No sooner had the township acquired a charter of freedom or certain immunities than a new antagonism showed itself between the ancient corporation of the city and the trade-guilds, these representing the later accretions. The territorial lord (if any) now sided, usually though not always, with the patrician party. But the guilds, nevertheless, succeeded in ultimately wresting many of the leading public offices from the exclusive possession of the patrician families. Meanwhile the leading men of the guilds had become *hommes arrivés*. They had acquired wealth, and influence which was in many cases hereditary in their family, and by the beginning of the sixteenth century they were confronted with the more or less veiled and more or less open opposition of the smaller guildsmen and of the newest comers into the city, the shiftless proletariat of serfs and free peasants, whom economic pressure was fast driving within the walls, but who, owing to the civic organisation having become crystallised, could no longer be absorbed into it. To this mass may be added a certain number of impoverished burghers, who, although nominally within the town organisation, were oppressed by the wealth of the magnates, plebeian and patrician.

The number of persons who, owing to the decay, or one might almost say the collapse, of the strength of the feudal system, were torn from the old moorings and left to drift about shiftless in a world utterly unprepared to deal with such an increase of what was practically vagabondage, was augmenting with every year. The vagrants in all Western European countries had never been so numerous as in the earlier part of the sixteenth century. A portion of these disinherited persons entered the service of kings and princes as mercenary soldiers, and thus became the first germ of the modern standing army. Another portion entered the begging profession, which now notably on the Continent became organised in orthodox and traditional form into guilds, each of which had its master and other officers. Yet another portion sought a more or less permanent domicile as journeymen craftsmen and unskilled labourers in the cities. This fact is noteworthy as the first indication of the proletariat in modern history. "It will be seen," says Friedrich Engels,[3] "that the plebeian opposition of the then towns consisted of very mixed elements. It united the degenerate components of the old feudal and guild organisation with the as yet undeveloped and new-born proletarian element of modern bourgeois society in embryo. Impoverished guildsmen there were, who through their privileges were still connected with the existing civic order on the one side, and serving-men out of place who had not as yet become proletarians on the other. Between the two were the "companions" (*Gesellen*) for the nonce outside the official society, and in their position resembling the proletariat as much as was possible in the then state of industry and under the existing guild-privilege. But, nevertheless, almost all of them were future guild-masters by virtue of this very guild-privilege."[4] A noteworthy feature of municipal life at this time was the difficulty and expense attendant on entry into the city organisation even for the status of simple citizen, still more for that of a guildsman. Within a few decades this had enormously increased.

The guild was a characteristic of all mediaeval life. On the model of the village-community, which was originally based on the notion of kinship, every interest, craft, and group of men formed itself into a "brotherhood" or "guild". The idea of individual autonomy, of individual action independent altogether of the community, is a modern idea which never entered the mediaeval mind. As we have above remarked, even the mendicants and vagabonds could not conceive of adopting begging as a career except under the auspices of a beggars' guild. The guild was not like a modern commercial syndicate, an abstract body united only by the thread of one immediate personal interest, whose members did not even know each other. His guild-membership interpenetrated the whole life, religious, convivial, social and political, of the mediaeval man. The guilds were more or less of the nature of masonic societies, whose concerns were by no means limited to the mere trade-function that appeared on the surface. "Business" had not as yet begun to absorb the whole life of men. The craft or "mystery" was a function intimately interwoven with the whole concrete social existence. But it is interesting to observe among the symptoms of transition characterising the sixteenth century, as noted above, the formation of companies of merchants apart from and outside the old guild-organisation. These latter really seem a kind of foreshadowing of the rings, trusts, and joint-stock companies of our own day. Many and bitter were the complaints of the manner in which prices were forced up by these earliest examples of the capitalistic syndicate, which powerfully contributed to the accumulation of wealth at one end of the scale and to the intensification of poverty at the other.[5]

The rich burgher loved nothing better than to display an ostentatious profusion of wealth in his house, in his dress, and in his entertainments. On the clothing and ornamentation of himself and his family he often squandered what might have been for his ancestor of the previous century the fortune of a lifetime. Especially was this the case at the Reichstags and other imperial assemblies held in the various free cities at which all the three feudal estates of the Empire were represented. It was the aim of the wealthy councillor or guild-master on these occasions to outbid the princes of the Empire in the magnificence of his person and establishment. The prince did not like to be outdone, and learnt to accustom himself to luxuries, and thereby to indefinitely increase his own expenditure. The same with all classes.

The knighthood or smaller nobles, no longer content with homely fare, sought after costly clothing, expensive food and exotic wines, and to approach the affluent furnishing of the city magnate. His one or two horses, his armour, sword and his lance, his homespuns made almost invariably on his estates, the wine grown in the neighbourhood, his rough oatmeal bread, 'the constituents of which had been ground at his own mill, the venison and wild fowl hunted by himself or by his few retainers, no longer sufficed for the knight's wants. In order to compass his new requirements he had to set to work in two ways. Formerly he had little or no need of money. He received, as he gave, everything in kind. Now that he had to deal with the beginnings of a world-market, money was a prime necessity. The first and most obvious way of getting it was to squeeze the peasant on his estate, who, bitten by the new mania, had also begun to accumulate and turn into cash the surplus products of labour on his holding. From what we have before said of the ways and manners of the knighthood, the reader may well imagine that he did not hesitate to "tower" the recalcitrant peasant, as it was called, that is, to throw him into his castle-dungeon if other means failed to make him disgorge his treasure as soon as it came to his lord's ears that he had any. But the more ordinary method of squeezing the peasant was by doubling and trebling the tithes and other dues, by imposing fresh burdens (many of them utterly unwarranted by custom) on any or no pretext. The princes, lay and ecclesiastic, applied the same methods on a more extended scale. These were often effected in an ingenious manner by the ecclesiastical lords through the forging of manorial rolls.

The second of the methods spoken of for "raising the wind" was the mortgaging of castle and lands to the money-lending syndicates of the towns, or, in the case of the greater princes, to the towns themselves in their corporate capacity. The Jews also came in for share of land mortgages. There were, in fact, few free or semi-free peasants whose lands were not more or less hypothecated. Meanwhile prices rose to an incredible extent in a few years.

Such were the causes and results of the change in domestic life which the economic evolution of the close of the Middle ages was now bringing about amongst all classes.

The ecclesiastical lords, or lords spiritual, differed in no way in their character and conduct from the temporal princes of the Empire. In one respect they outdid the princes, namely, in the forgery of documents, as already mentioned. Luxury had, moreover, owing to the communication which they had with Rome and thus indirectly with the Byzantine civilisation, already begun with the prelates in the earlier Middle Ages. It now burst all bounds. The ecclesiastical courts were the seat of every kind of debauchery. As we shall see later on, they also became they places where the new learning first flourished. But in addition to the general luxury in which the higher ecclesiastics outdid the lay element of the Empire, there was a special cause which rendered them obnoxious alike to the peasants, to the towns, and to their own feudatory nobles. This special cause was the enormous sum payable to Rome for the Pallium or Investiture, a tax that had to be raised by the inhabitants of the diocese on every change of archbishop, bishop, or abbot. In addition thereto the entire income of the first year after the investiture accrued to the Papal Treasury under the name of Annates. This constituted a continuous drain on the ecclesiastical dependencies and indirectly on the whole Empire. There must also be added the cost of frequent journeys to Rome, where each dignitary during his residence held court in a style of sumptuous magnificence. All these expenses tended to drain the resources of the territories held as spiritual fiefs in a more onerous degree than happened to other territories. Moreover, the system of the sale of indulgences or remissions for all sins committed up to date was now being prosecuted to an extent never heard of before with a view to meet the increased expenditure of the Papal See, and especially the cost of completing the cathedral of St. Peter's at Rome. Thus by a sort of voluntary tax the wealth of German was still further transferred to Italy. Hence can readily be seen the reason of the venomous hatred which among all classes of the Empire had been gradually accumulating towards the Papacy for more than a generation, and which ultimately found expression in Luther's fulminations.

The peasant of the period was of three kinds the *leibegener* or serf, who was little letter than a slave, who cultivated his lord's domain, upon whom unlimited burdens might be fixed, and who was in all respects amenable to the will of his lord; the *höriger* or villein, whose services were limited alike in kind and amount; and the *freier* or free peasant, who merely paid what was virtually a quit-rent in kind or in money for being allowed to retain his holding or status in the rural community under the protection of the manorial lord. The last was practically the counterpart of the mediaeval English copyholder. The Germans had undergone essentially the same transformations in social organisation as the other populations of Europe.

The barbarian nations at the time of their great migration in the fifth century were organised on a tribal and village basis. The head man was simply *primus inter pares.* In the course of their wanderings the successful military leader acquired powers and assumed a position that was unknown to the previous times, when war, such as it was, was merely inter-tribal and inter-clannish, and did not involve the movements of peoples and federations of tribes, and when, in consequence, the need for permanent military leaders or for the semblance of a military hierarchy had not arisen. The military leader now placed himself at the head of the older social organisation, and associated with his immediate followers on terms approaching equality. A well-known illustration of this is the incident of the vase taken from the Cathedral of Rheims, and of Chlodowig's efforts to rescue it from his independent comrades-in-arms.

The process of the development of the feudal polity of the Middle Ages is, of course, a very complicated one, owing to the various strands that go to compose it. In addition to the German tribes themselves, who moved *en masse,* carrying with them their tribal and village organisation, under the over-lordship of the various military leaders, were the indigenous inhabitants amongst whom they settled. The latter in the country districts, even in many of the territories within the Roman Empire, still largely retained the primitive communal organisation. The new-comers, therefore, found in the rural communities a social system already in existence into which they naturally fitted, but as an aristocratic body over against the conquered inhabitants. The latter, though not all reduced to a servile condition, nevertheless held their land from the conquering body under conditions which constituted them an order of freemen inferior to the newcomers.

To put the matter briefly, the military leaders developed into barons and princes, and in some cases the nominal centralisation culminated as in France and England in the kingly office; while, in Germany and Italy, it took the form of the revived imperial office, the spiritual over-lord of the whole of Christendom being the Pope, who had his vassals in the prince-prelates and subordinate ecclesiastical holders. In addition to the princes sprung originally from the military leaders of the migratory nations, there were their free followers, who developed ultimately into the knighthood or inferior nobility; the inhabitants of the conquered districts forming a distinct class of inferior freemen or of serfs. But the essentially personal relation with which the whole process started soon degenerated into one based on property. The most primitive form of property — land — was at the outset what was termed allodial, at least among the conquering race, from every social group having the possession, under the trusteeship of its head man, of the land on which it settled. Now, owing to the necessities of the time, owing to the need of protection, to violence and to religious motives, it passed into the hands of the over-lord, temporal or spiritual, as his possession; and the inhabitants, even in the case of populations which had not been actually conquered, became his vassals, villeins, or serfs, as the case might be. The process by means of which this was accomplished was more or less gradual; indeed, the entire extinction of communal rights, whereby the notion of private ownership is fully realised, was not universally effected even in the west of Europe till within a measurable distance of our own time.[6]

From the foregoing it will be understood that the

oppression of the peasant, under the feudalism of the Middle Ages, and especially of the later Middle Ages, was viewed by him as an infringement of his rights. During the period of time constituting mediaeval history the peasant, though he often slumbered, yet often started up to a sudden consciousness of his position. The memory of primitive communism was never quite extinguished, and the continual peasant-revolts of the Middle Ages, though immediately occasioned, probably, by some fresh invasion, by which it was sought to tear from the "common man" yet another shred of his surviving rights, always had in the background the ideal, vague though it may have been, of his ancient freedom. Such, undoubtedly, was the meaning of the Jacquerie in France, with its wild and apparently senseless vengeance; of the Wat Tyler revolt in England, with its systematic attempt to embody the vague tradition of the primitive village community in the legends of the current ecclesiastical creed; of the numerous revolts in Flanders and North Germany; of the Hussite movement in Bohemia, under Ziska; of the rebellion led by George Doza in Hungary; and, as we shall see in the body of the present work, of the social movements of Reformation Germany, in which, with the partial exception of Ket's rebellion in England a few years later, we may consider them as coming to an end.

For the movements in question were distinctly the last of their kind. The civil wars of religion in France, and the great rebellion in England against Charles the First, which also assumed a religious colouring, open a new era in popular revolts. In the latter, particularly, we have clearly before us the attempt of the new middle class of town and country, the independent citizen, and the now independent yeoman, to assert its supremacy over the old feudal estates or orders. The new conditions had swept away the revolutionary tradition of the mediaeval period, whose golden age lay in the past with its communal-holding and free men with equal rights on the basis of the village organisation — rights which with every century the peasant felt more and

26

more slipping away from him. The place of this tradition was now taken by an ideal of individual freedom, apart from any social bond, and on a basis merely political, the way for which had been prepared by that very conception of individual proprietorship on the part of the landlord, against which the older revolutionary sentiment had protested. A most powerful instrument in accommodating men's minds to this change of view, in other words, to the establishment of the new individualistic principle, was the Roman or Civil law, which, at the period dealt with in the present book, had become the basis whereon disputed points were settled in the Imperial Courts. In this respect also, though to a lesser extent, may be mentioned the Canon or Ecclesiastical law, — consisting of papal decretals on various points which were founded partially on the Roman or Civil law, — a juridical system which also fully and indeed almost exclusively recognised the individual holding of property as the basis of civil society (albeit not without a recognition of social duties on the part of the owner).

Learning was now beginning to differentiate itself from the ecclesiastical profession, and to become a definite vocation in its various branches. Crowds of students flocked to the seats of learning, and, as travelling scholars, earned a precarious living by begging or "professing" medicine, assisting the illiterate for a small fee, or working wonders, such as casting horoscopes, or performing thaumaturgic tricks. The professors of law were now the most influential members of the Imperial Council and of the various Imperial Courts. In Central Europe, as elsewhere, notably in France, the civil lawyers were always on the side of the centralising power, alike against the local jurisdictions and against the peasantry.

The effects of the conquest of Constantinople in 1453, and the consequent dispersion of the accumulated Greek learning of the Byzantine Empire, had, by the end of the fifteenth century, begun to show themselves in a notable modification of European culture. The circle of the seven sciences, the Quadrivium, and the

Trivium, in other words, the medieval system of learning, began to be antiquated. Scholastic philosophy, that is to say, the controversy of the Scotists and the Thomists, was now growing out of date. Plato was extolled at the expense of Aristotle. Greek, and even Hebrew, was eagerly sought after. Latin itself was assuming another aspect; the Renaissance Latin is classical Latin, whilst Mediaval Latin is dog-Latin. The physical universe now began to be inquired into with a perfectly fresh interest, but the inquiries were still conducted under the aegis of the old habits of thought. The universe was still a system of mysterious affinities and magical powers to the investigator of the Renaissance period, as it had been before. There was this difference, however: it was now attempted to *systematise* the magical theory of the universe. While the common man held a store of traditional magical beliefs respecting the natural world, the learned man deduced these beliefs from the Neo-Platonists, from the Kabbala, from Hermes Trismegistos, and from a variety of other sources, and attempted to arrange this somewhat heterogeneous mass of erudite lore into a system of organised thought.

The Humanistic movement, so called, the movement, that is, of revived classical scholarship, had already begun in Germany before what may be termed the *sturm und drang,* of the Renaissance proper. Foremost among the exponents of this older Humanism, which dates from the middle of the fifteenth century, were Nicholas of Cusa and his disciples, Rudolph Agricola, Alexander Hegius and Jacob Wimpheling. But the new Humanism and the new Renaissance movement generally throughout Northern Europe centred chiefly in two personalities, Johannes Reuchlin and Desiderius Erasmus. Reuchlin was the founder of the new Hebrew learning, which up till then had been exclusively confined to the synagogue. It was he who unlocked the mysteries of the Kabbala to the Gentile world. But though it is for his introduction of Hebrew study that Reuchlin is best known to posterity, yet his services in the diffusion and popularisation of classical culture were enormous. The dispute of

Reuchlin with the ecclesiastical authorities at Cologne excited literary Germany from end to end. It was the first general skirmish of the new and the old spirit in Central and Northern Europe. But the man who was destined to become the personification of the Humanist movement, as the new learning was called, was Erasmus. The illegitimate son of the daughter of a Rotterdam burgher, he early became famous on account of his erudition, in spite of the adverse circumstances of his youth. Like all the scholars of his time, he passed rapidly from one country to another, settling finally in Basel, then at the height of its reputation as a literary and typographical centre. The whole intellectual movement of the time centres round Erasmus, as is particularly noticeable in the career of Ulrich von Hutten, dealt with in the course of this history. As instances of the classicism of the period, we may note the uniform change of the patronymic into the classical equivalent, or some classicism supposed to be the equivalent. Thus the name Erasmus itself was a classicism of his father's name Gerhard, the German name Muth became Mutianus, Trittheim became Trithemius, Schwarzerd became Melanchthon, and so on.

We have spoken of the other side of the intellectual movement of the period. This other side showed itself in mystical attempts at reducing nature to law in the light of the traditional problems which had been set, to wit, those of alchemy and astrology: the discovery of the philosopher's stone, of the transmutation of metals, of the elixir of life, and of the correspondences between the planets and terrestrial bodies. Among the most prominent exponents of these investigations may be mentioned Philippus von Hohenheim or Paracelsus, and Cornelius Agrippa of Nettesheiin, in Germany, Nostrodamus, in France, and Cardanus, in Italy. These men represented a tendency which was pursued by thousands in the learned world. It was a tendency which had the honour of being the last in history to embody itself in a distinct mythical cycle. "Doctor Faustus" may probably have had a historical germ; but in any case "Doctor

Faustus," as known to legend and to literature, is merely a personification of the practical side of the new learning. The minds of men were waking up to interest in nature. There was one man, Copernicus, who, at least partially, struck through the traditionary atmosphere in which nature was enveloped, and to his insight we owe the foundation of astronomical science; but otherwise the whole intellectual atmosphere was charged with occult views. In fact, the learned world of the sixteenth century would have found itself quite at home in the pretensions and fancies of our *fin de siècle* theosophists, with their notions of making miracles non-miraculous, of reducing the marvellous to being merely the result of penetration on the part of certain seers and investigators of the secret powers of nature. Every wonder-worker was received with open arms by learned and unlearned alike. The possibility of producing that which was out of the ordinary range of natural occurrences was not seriously doubted by any. Spells and enchantments, conjurations, calculations of nativities, were matters earnestly investigated at universities and courts. There were, of course, persons who were ever to detect impostors: and amongst them some of the most zealous votaries of the occult arts — for example, Trittheim and the learned Humanist, Conrad Muth or Mutianus, both of whom professed to have regarded Faust as a fraud. But this did not imply any disbelief in the possibility of the alleged pretensions. In the Faust-myth is embodied, moreover, the opposition between the new learning on its physical side and the old religious faith. The theory that the investigation of the mysteries of nature had in it something sinister and diabolical which had been latent throughout the Middle Ages was brought into especial prominence by the new religious movements. The popular feeling that the line between natural magic and the black art was somewhat doubtful, that the one had a tendency to shade off into the other, now received fresh stimulus. The notion of compacts with the devil was a familiar one, and that it should be resorted to for the purpose of acquiring an acquaintance with hidden lore and magical powers seemed quite natural.

It will have already been seen from what we have said that the religious revolt was largely economical in its causes. The intense hatred, common alike to the smaller nobility, the burghers and the peasants, of the ecclesiastical hierarchy, was obviously due to its ever-increasing exactions. The sudden increase in the sale of indulgences, like the proverbial last straw, broke down the whole system; but any other incident might have served the purpose equally well. The prince-prelates were, in some instances, at the outset, not averse to the movement; they would not have been indisposed to have converted their territories into secular fiefs of the Empire. It was only after this hope had been abandoned that they definitely took sides with the Papal authority.

The opening of the sixteenth century thus presents to us medieval society, social, political and religious, "run to seed". The feudal organisation was outwardly intact; the peasant, free and bond, formed the foundation; above him came the knighthood or inferior nobility; parallel with them was the *Ehrbarkeit* of the less important towns, holding from mediate lordship; above these towns came the free cities, which held immediately from the Empire, organised into three bodies, a governing Council in which the *Ehrbarkeit* usually predominated, where they did not entirely compose it, a Common Council composed of the masters of the various guilds, and the General Council of the free citizens. Those journeymen, whose condition was fixed from their being outside the guild-organisations, usually had guilds of their own. Above the free cities in the social pyramid stood the Princes of the Empire, lay and ecclesiastic, with the Electoral College, or the seven Electoral Princes, forming their head. These constituted the feudal "estates" of the Empire. Then came the King of the Romans; and, as the apex of the whole, the Pope in one function and the Emperor in another crowned the edifice. The supremacy, not merely of the Pope, but of the complementary temporal head of the medieval polity, the Emperor, was acknowledged in a shadowy way, even in countries such as France and England, which had no direct connection with the Empire. For, as the spiritual power was also temporal, so the temporal political power had, like everything else in the Middle Ages, a quasi-religious significance.

The minds of men in speculative matters, in theology, in philosophy, and in jurisprudence, were outgrowing the old doctrines, at least in their old forms. In theology the notion of salvation by the faith of the individual, and not through the fact of belonging to a corporate organisation, which was the mediaeval conception, was latent in the minds of multitudes of religious persons before expression was given to it by Luther. The aversion to scholasticism, bred by the revived knowledge of the older Greek philosophies in the original, produced a curious amalgam; but scholastic habits of thought were still dominant through it all. The new theories of nature amounted to little more than old superstitions, systematised and reduced to rule, though here and there the later physical science, based on observation and experiment, peeped through. In jurisprudence the epoch is marked by the final conquest of the Roman civil law, in its spirit, where not in its forms, over the old customs, pre-feudal and feudal. This motley world of decayed knights, lavish princes, oppressed and rebellious peasants, turbulent townsmen, licentious monks and friars, mendicant scholars and hireling soldiers, is the world some of whose least known aspects we are about to consider in the following pages.

Footnotes

1. We are here, of course, dealing more especially with Germany; but substantially the same course was followed in the development of municipalities in other parts of Europe.

2. *Einleitung,* pp. 255, 256.

3. *Der Bauernkrieg,* p.31

4. The three grades in the craft-guilds were those of apprentice, companion, and master. Every guildsman was supposed to pass through them.

5. See Appendix A.

6. Cf. Von Maurer's *Einleitung zur Geschichte der Mark-Verfassung;* Gomme's *Village Communities;* Stubbs' *Constitutional History.*

I. First Signs of Social and Religious Revolt

The echoes of the Hussite movement in Bohemia spread far and wide through Central Europe at the beginning of the fifteenth century. It was not in vain that Ziska bequeathed his skin for the purposes of a drum, since the echoes of its beating made themselves heard for many a year in Bohemia and throughout Central Europe. The disciples of the movement settled in different countries, and became centres of propaganda, and the movement attached itself to the peasants' discontent. Amid the various stirrings that took place, there are one or two that may arrest our attention owing to their importance and their typical character.

It was in the year 1476, when Rudolph of Scherenberg occupied the Episcopal See of Würzburg, that a cowherd, named Hans Boheim, of the neighbouring village of Niklashausen, who was accustomed to pipe and to drum at local festivities, at places on the banks of the little stream called the Tauber, was suddenly seized with an inspiration of preaching for the conversion of his neighbours from their sins. It appeared to him that his life had been hitherto sinful; he gave up all participation in village feasts, he became a dreamer and announced that he had had visions of the Virgin. In the middle of Lent he proclaimed that he had been given a divine mission from the Mother of God herself to burn his pipe and drum and to devote himself entirely to preaching the Gospel to the common man. All were to abandon their former way of life, were to lay aside all personal ornament, and in humble attire to perform pilgrimages to Nihkashausen, and there worship the Virgin as they esteemed their souls' salvation. In all this there was nothing very alarming to the authorities. Peasantly inspirations were by no means unknown in the Middle Ages; but the matter assumed another aspect when the new seer, Hans Pfeifferlein, or "the little piper" as he was nicknamed, announced that the Queen of Heaven had revealed to him that there should henceforth be neither Emperor, Pope, Prince, nor any lay or spiritual authority; but that all men should be brothers, earning their bread by the sweat of their brows, and sharing alike in all things. There were to be no more imposts or dues; land, woods, pastures, and water were to be free. The new Gospel struck root immediately. The peasant folk streamed to Niklashausen, from all sides, men and women, young and old, journeymen, lads from the plough, girls from the fields, their sickles in their hands, without leave of lord or master, and without preparation of ally sort whatever. Food and the necessary clothing; and shelter were given them by those on the way who had already embraced the: new Kingdom of God. The universal greeting, among the pilgrims was "brother" and "sister".

This went on for some months, the young prophet choosing chiefly Sundays and holidays for his harangues Ignorant even of writing, he was backed by the priest of Niklashausen, and by perhaps two or three other influential persons. Many were the offerings brought to the Niklashausen shrine. Well nigh all who journeyed thither left some token behind, were it only a rough peasant's cap or a wax candle, Those who could afford it gave costly clothing and jewellery. The proclamation of universal equality was indeed a Gospel that appealed to the common man; the resumption of their old rights, the release from every form of oppression, as a proclamation from heaven itself, were tidings to him of great joy. The prophetic youth was hailed by all as the new Messiah. After each week's sermon he invited the congregation to return next week with redoubled numbers; and his commands were invariably obeyed. Men, women and children fell on their knees before him, crying: "Oh, man of God, sent from heaven, have mercy on us and pity us". They tore the wool threads from his shaggy sheepskin cap, regarding them as sacred relics. The priests of the surrounding districts averred that he was a sorcerer and devil-possessed, and that a wizard had appeared to him, clad in white, in the form of the Virgin, and had instilled into

36

him the pernicious doctrines he was preaching. In all the surrounding country his miracles were talked about. The Bishops of Mainz and Würzburg and the Council of Nürnberg forbade their villeins, under heavy penalties, from making the pilgrimage to Niklashausen. But the effect of such measures only lasted for a short time.

Finally, on the Sunday before the day of Saint Kilian, Hans Boheim, on the conclusion of his discourse, invited his hearers, as usual, to come on the next occasion. This time, however, he ordered men only to appear, but with arms and ammunition; women and children were to be left at home. No sooner did the tidings of this turn of affairs reach the ears of the Bishop at Würzburg than the latter resolved to forestall the movement. He sent thirty-four mounted men-at-arms after nightfall to Niklashausen; they burst upon the sleeping youth, tore him from the house where he lay, and hurried him to Würzburg, bound on horseback. But as it was near the end of the week, 4000 pilgrims had already arrived at Niklashausen, and, on hearing the news of the attack, they hurried after the marauders, and caught them up close by the Castle of Würzburg. One of the knights was wounded, but his comrades succeeded in carrying him within the walls. The peasants failed to effect the intended rescue. By the Sunday, 34,000 peasants had assembled at Niklashausen; but the report of the capture of Boheim had a depressing effect, and several thousands returned home. There were nevertheless some among the bands who, instigated probably by Boheim's friend, the parish priest of Niklashausen, endeavoured to rally the remaining multitude and incite them to a new attempt at rescue. One of them alleged that the Holy Trinity had appeared to him, and commanded that they should proceed with their pilgrim candles in their hands to the Castle of Würzburg, that the doors would open of themselves, and that their prophet would walk out to greet them. About 16,000 followed these leaders, marching many hours through the night, and arriving early nest morning at the castle with flaming candles, and armed with the roughest weapons. Kunz von Thunfeld, a decayed knight, and Michael, his son, constituted themselves the leaders of the motley band. The marshal of the castle received their, demanding their pleasure. "We require the holy youth," said the peasants. "Surrender him to us, and all will be well; refuse, and we will use force." On the marshal's hesitating in his answer, he was greeted with a shower of stones, which drove him to seek safety within the walls. The bishop opened fire on the peasants, but after a short time sent one of his knights to announce that the cause of their preacher would be duly considered at a proper time and place, conjuring them at the same time to depart immediately in accordance with their vows. By cajolery and threats he succeeded in his object; the bands raised the siege of the castle, and dispersed homewards in straggling parties. The ruffianly scoundrel no sooner observed that the unsuspecting peasants were quietly wending their way home in small bodies, without a thought of hostilities, than he ordered his knights to pursue them, to attack them in the rear, and to murder or capture the ringleaders. The poor people, nevertheless, defended themselves with courage against this cowardly onslaught; twelve of them were left dead on the spot; many of the remainder sought shelter in the church of the neighbouring village. Threatened there with fire and sword, they surrendered, and were brought back to Würzburg and thrown into the dungeons of the castle. The majority were liberated before long; but the peasant who was alleged to have received the vision of the Holy Trinity, as well as he who had wounded the knight on the occasion of the attempt at rescue a few days before, were detained in prison, and on the following Friday were beheaded outside the castle. Hans Boheim was at the same time burned to ashes. The leader of the revolt, Kunz von Thunfeld, a feudatory of the bishop, fled the territory, and was only allowed to return on his formally surrendering his lands in perpetuity to the bishopric. Such was the history of a movement that may be reckoned as one of the more direct forerunners of the peasants' war.

In the years 1491 and 1492 occurred the rising of the oppressed and plundered villeins of the Abbot of Kempten. The ecclesiastics on this domain had exhausted every possible means of injuring the unfortunate peasants, and numbers of free villeins had been converted into serfs by means of forged documents. The immediate cause of the revolt, however, was the seizure, by the abbot, of the stock of wine of a peasant who had just died, in addition to the horse which he was empowered to claim. An onslaught was made by the infuriated peasants on the monastery, and the abbot had to retire to his stronghold, the Castle of Liebenthann, hard by. The Emperor ultimately intervened, and effected a compromise. But the first organised peasant movement took place in Elsass[1] in 1493, and comprised burghers as well as peasants among its numbers. They were for the most part feudatories of the Bishop of Strassburg. By devious paths the members of this secret organisation were wont to betake themselves to the hill of Hungerberg, northwest of the little town of Schlettstadt. The ostensible objects of the association were complete freedom for the common man, reformation of the Church in the: sense that no priest should have more than one benefice, the introduction of a year of jubilee, in which all debts should be abolished, the extinction of all tithes, dues and other burdens, and the abolition of the spiritual courts and the territorial juridical court at Rothweil. A *Judenhetze* also appears amongst the articles. The leader of this movement was one Jacob Wimpfeling. The programme and plan of action was to seize the town of Schlettstadt, to plunder the monastery there, and then by forced marches to spread themselves over all Elsass, surprising one town after another. It would seem that this was the first peasant movement that received the name of *Bundschuh*, and the almost superstitious importance attached to the sign of this hind emblazoned on the flag is characteristic of the Middle Ages. The banner was the result of careful deliberations, and the final decision was that as the knight was distinguished by his spurs, so the peasant rising to obtain justice for his class should take as his emblem the common shoe he was accustomed to wear, laced from the ankle up to the knee with leathern thongs. They fondly hoped that the moment this banner was displayed, all capable of fighting would flock to the standard, from the villages and smaller towns.

Just as all was prepared for the projected stroke, the *Bundschuh* shared the common fate of similar movements, and was betrayed; and this in spite of the terrible threats that were held out to all joining, in the event of their turning traitors. It must be admitted that there was much folly in the manner in which many persons were enrolled, and this may have led to the speedy betrayal. Everybody who was suspected of having an inkling of the movement was forced to swear allegiance to the secret league. Immediately on the betrayal, bodies of knights scoured the country, mercilessly seizing all suspected of belonging to the conspiracy, and dragging them to the nearest tribunal, where they were tortured and finally quartered alive or hung. Many of the fugitives succeeded in taking refuge in Switzerland, where they seem to have been kindly welcomed. But the *Bundschuh* only slept, it was by no means extinguished.

In the year 1502 nine years later, the bishopric of *Speyer*, the court of which was noted for its extravagance and tyranny, had to face another *Bundschuh*. This second movement had able men at its head, and extended over well nigh all the regions of the Upper and Middle Rhine. It similarly took the nature of a conspiracy, rather than of an open rebellion. Within a few weeks, 7000 men and 400 women had been sworn into the league, from a large number of villages, hamlets and small towns, for the larger towns were purposely left out, the movement being essentially a peasant one. The village and *mark* of Untergrünbach was its centre. Its object and aim was nothing less than the complete overthrow of the existing ecclesiastical and feudal organisation of the Empire. The articles of the association declared: "We have joined ourselves together in order that we may be free. We will free ourselves with arms in our hands, for we would be as the Swiss. We will root out and abolish all authorities and lordships from the land, and march against them with the force of our host and with well-armed hand under our banner. And all who do not honour and acknowledge us shall be killed. The princes and nobles broken and done with, we will storm the clergy in their foundations and abbeys. We will overpower them, and hunt out and hill all priests and monks together." The property of the clergy and the nobles was to be seized and divided; as in the former case, all feudal dues were to be abolished, the primitive communism in the use of the land, and of what was on it, was to be resumed. The pass-word, by means of which the members of the organisation were known to one another, was the answer to the question:

"How fares it?" The question and answer were in the form of a rhyme:-

"Loset! Was ist nun fur ein Wesen? "

"Wir mögen vor Pfaffen und Adel nit genesen."

This may be paraphrased as follows:-

"Well, now! And how doth it fare?"

"Of priests and of nobles we've enough and to spare."

The idea was to rise at the opportune moment, as the Swiss had done, to free themselves of all intermediate lordship, and to recognise no master below the king of the Romans and the Emperor. "Nought but the justice of God "was the motto of their flag, and their colours were white and blue. Before the figure of a crucifix a peasant knelt, and below was depicted a great *Bundschuh*, the sign which had now become established as the symbol of the peasants' movements. With consummate tact, the leaders of the revolt forbade any members to go to confession, and it was the disregard of this order that led to the betrayal of the cause. A peasant in confession revealed the secret to a priest, who

41

in his turn revealed it to the authorities. Ecclesiastics, princes, and nobles at once took their measures. The most barbarous persecution and punishment of all suspected of having been engaged in the *Bundschuh* conspiracy followed. Those concerned had their property confiscated, their wives and children were driven from the country, and they themselves were in many, cases quartered alive; the more prominent men, by a refinement of cruelty, being dragged to the place of execution tied to a horse's tail. A tremendous panic seized all the privileged classes, from the Emperor to the knight. They earnestly discussed the situation in no less than three separate assemblies of the estates. Large numbers of those involved in this second *Bundschuh* managed to escape, owing to the pluck and loyalty of the peasants. A few bands were hastily got together, and, although quite insufficient to effect a successful revolt, they were able to keep the knightly warriors and *landesknechte* at bay at certain critical points, so as to give the men who had really been the life and intelligence of the movement time to escape into Switzerland or into other territories where they were unknown. In some cases the secret was so well kept that the local organisers remained unnoticed even in their own villages.

For ten years after the collapse of the second *Bundschuh* in the Rhenish district, the peasants remained quiet. It was not till 1512 that things began again to stir. One of the leaders, who had escaped notice on the suppression of the former conspiracy, was Joss Fritz. He was himself a native of Untergrünbach, which had been its seat. He there acted as *Bannwart* or ranger of the district lands. For nearly ten years Joss wandered about from country to country, but amid all his struggles for existence he never forgot the *Bundschuh*. Joss was a handsome man, of taking and even superior manners. He was very careful in his dress, sometimes apparelling himself in black jerkin with white hose, sometimes in red with yellow hose, sometimes in drab with green hose. He would seem to have been at one time a *landesknecht,* and had certainly taken part in various campaigns in a military capacity.

Whether it was from his martial bearing or the engaging nature of his personality, it is evident that Joss Fritz was in his way a born leader of men. About 1512 Joss settled down in a village called Lehen, a few miles from the town of Freiburg, in Breisgau. Here he again obtained the position of *Bannwart,* and here he began to seriously gather together the scattered threads of the old movement, and to collect recruits. He went to work cautiously; first of all confining himself to general complaints of the degeneracy of the times in the village tavern, or before the doors of the cottagers on summer evenings. He soon became the centre of an admiring group of swains, who looked up to him as the much-travelled man of the world, who eagerly sought his conversation, and who followed his counsel in their personal affairs.

As Joss saw that he was obtaining the confidence of his neighbours, his denunciations of the evils of the time grew more earnest and impassioned. At the same time he threw out hints as to the ultimate outcome of the existing state of things. But it was only after many months that he ventured to broach the real purpose of his life. One day when they were all assembled round him, he hinted that he might be able to tell them something to their advantage, would they but pledge themselves to secrecy. He then took each individually, and after calming the man's conscience with the assurance that the proposal for which he claimed strict secrecy was an honourable one, he expounded his plan of an organisation of all the oppressed, an undertaking which he claimed to be in full accord with Holy Writ. He never insisted upon an immediate adhesion, but preferred to leave his man to think the matter over.

Joss would sometimes visit his neighbours in their houses, explaining to them how all ancient custom, right and tradition was being broken through to gratify the rapacity of the ruling classes. He put forward as the objects of the undertaking the suppression of the payment of interest after it had amounted to an equivalent of the original sum lent; also that no one was to be

43

required to give more than one day's service per year to his lord. "We will," he declared, "govern ourselves according to our old rights and traditions, of which we have been forcibly and wrongfully deprived by our masters. Thou knowest well," he would continue, "how long we have been laying our claims before the Austrian Government at Ensisheim".[2]

From speaking of small grievances, Joss was gradually led to develop his scheme for the overthrow of feudalism, and for the establishment of what was tantamount to primitive conditions. At the same time he gave his hearers a rendezvous at a certain hour of eventide in a meadow, called the *Hardmatte*, which lay outside the village, and skirted a wood. The stillness of the hour, broken only by the sounds of nature hushing herself to rest for the night, was, at the time appointed, invaded by the eager talk of groups of villagers. All his little company assembled, Joss Fritz here, for the first time, fully developed his schemes. In future, said he, we must see that we have no other lords than God, the Pope, and the Emperor; the Court at Rothweil, he said, must he abolished; each must be able to obtain justice in his native village, and no churchman must he allowed to hold more than one benefice; the superfluity of the monasteries must be distributed amongst the poor; the dues and imposts with which the peasants are burdened must he removed; a permanent peace must he established throughout Christendom, as the perpetual feuds of the nobles meant destruction and misery for the peasants; finally, the primitive communism in woods, pasture, water, and the chase must be restored.

Joss Fritz's proposals struck a sympathetic chord in the hearts of his hearers. It was only when he wound up by insisting upon the necessity of forming a new *Bundschuh* that some few of them hung back and went to obtain the advice of the village priest on the matter. Father John (such was his name was, however, in full accord in his ideas with Joss, and answered that the proposals were indeed a godly thing, the success of which was foretold in the Scriptures themselves.

The meetings on the *Hardmatte* led to the formation of a kind of committee, composed of those who were most devoted to the cause. These were Augustin Enderlin, Kilian Mayer, Hans Freuder, Hans and Karius Heitz, Peter Stublin, Jacob Hauser, Hans Hummel — Hummel hailed from the neighbourhood of Stuttgart — and Hieronymus, who was also a stranger, a journeyman baker working at the mill of Lehen, who had travelled far, and had acquired a considerable fund of oratory. All these men were untiring in their exertions to obtain recruits for the new movement. After having prepared the latter's minds, they handed over the new-comers to Joss for deeper initiation, if he thought fit. It was not in crusades and pilgrimages he taught them, but in the *Bundschuh* that the "holy sepulchre" was to be obtained. The true "holy sepulchre" was to be found, namely, in the too long buried liberties of the people. The new *Bundschuh,* he maintained, had ramifications extending as far as Cologne, and embracing members from all orders.

Joss Fritz had indeed before coming to Lehen travelled through the Black Forest and the district of Speyer, in the attempt, by no means altogether unsuccessful, to reunite the crushed and scattered branches of the old *Bundschuh.* Among the friends he had made in this way was a poor knight of the name of Stoffel, of Freiburg. The latter travelled incessantly in the cause; he was always carefully dressed, and usually rode on a white horse. The missionaries of the *Bundschuh,* under the direction of Joss Fritz, assumed many different characters; now they were peasants, now townsmen, now decayed knights, according to the localities they visited. The organisation of the movement was carried out on lines which have been since reproduced in the Fenian rising. It was arranged in "circles," the members of which knew one another, but not those outside the "circle". Even the beggars' guild was pressed into the service, and very useful adjuncts the beggars were, owing to their nomadic habits. The heads of the "circles" communicated with each other at intervals as to the number of recruits and as to the morale of their members. They compared notes with the two leaders of the movement, Joss and his friend Stoffel, both of whom rode constantly from place to place to keep their workers up to the mark. The muster-roll would be held on these occasions, as at Lehen itself, after dark, and in some woodland glade, near the village. The village taverns, generally the kitchens of some better-to-do peasant, were naturally among the best recruiting grounds, and the hosts themselves were often heads of "circles". Strange and picturesque must have been these meetings after night-fall, when the members of the "circle" came together, the peasants in their plain blue or grey cloth and buff leather, the leaders in what to us seem the fantastic costumes of the period, red , stockings, trunk-hose and doublet slashed with bright yellow, or the whole dress of yellow slashed with black, the slouch hat, with ostrich feather, surmounting the whole; the short sword for the leaders, and a hoe or other agricultural implement for the peasant, constituted the arms of the company.

There was a visible sign by which the brethren recognised each other: it was a sign in the form of the letter H, of black stuff in a red field, sewn on to the breast-cloth. There appears also to have been another sign which certain of the members bore instead of the above; this consisted of three cross slits or slashes in the stuff of the right sleeve. This *Bundschuh,* like the previous one in Untergrünbach, had its countersign, which, to the credit of all concerned, be it said, was never revealed, and is not known to this day. The new *Bundschuh* was now thoroughly organised with all its officers, none of whom received money for their services.

The articles of association drawn up were the result of many nightly meetings on the *Hardmatte,* and embodied the main points insisted upon by Joss in his exhortations to the peasants. They included the abolition of all feudal powers. God, the Pope, and the Emperor were alone to be recognised as having authority. The Court at Rothweil and all the ecclesiastical courts were to be abolished, and justice relegated to the village council as of old. The interest payable on the debts of the mortgaged holdings of the peasants was to be discontinued. Fishing, hunting, woods and pasture were to be free to all. The clergy were to be limited to one benefice apiece. The monasteries and ecclesiastical foundations were to be curtailed, and their superfluous property confiscated. All feudal dues were to cease.

The strange and almost totemistic superstition that the mediaeval mind attached to symbolism is here, evinced by the paramount importance acquired by the question of the banner. A banner was costly, and the *Bundschuh* was poor, but the banner was the first necessity of every movement. In this case, it was obligatory that the banner should have a *Bundschuh* inscribed upon it. Artists of that time objected to painting *Bundschuhs* on banners; they were afraid to be compromised. Hence it was, above all things, necessary to have plenty of money wherewith to bribe some painter. Kilian Mayer gave five vats of wine to a baker, also one of the brotherhood, in Freiburg, to be sold in that town. The proceeds were brought to Joss as a contribution to the banner fund. Many another did similarly; some of those who met on the *Haydmatte,* however, objected to this tax. But ultimately Joss managed, by hook or by crook, to scrape together what was deemed needful. Joss then called upon a "brother" from it distant part of the country, one known to no one in Freiburg, to repair to the latter city and hunt up a painter. The "brother" was in a state of dire apprehension, and went to the house of the painter Friedrich, but at first appeared not to know for what he had come. With much hesitation, he eventually gasped out that he wanted a *Bundschuh* painted. Friedrich did not at, all like the proposal, and kicked the unfortunate peasant into the street, telling him not to come in future with such questionable orders. The artist instantly informed the Town Council of Freiburg of the occurrence; but as the latter did not know whence the mysterious personage had come, nor whither he had gone, they had to leave the matter in abeyance. They issued orders, however, for all true and faithful burghers to be on the look-out for further traces of the mischief.

After this failure, Joss bethought him that he had better

take the matter in hand himself. Now, there was another artist of Freiburg, by name Theodosius, who was just then painting frescoes in the church at Lehen; to him Joss went one evening with Hans Enderlin, a person of authority in the village, and Kilian Mayer. They invited him to the house of one of the party, and emptied many a measure of vine. When they had all drunk their fill, they went to walk in the garden, just as the stars were beginning to come out. Joss now approached the painter with his project. He told him that there was a stranger in the village who wanted a small banner painted and had asked him (Joss) to demand the cost. Theodosius showed himself amenable as regards this point, but wanted to know what was to be the device on the banner. Directly Joss mentioned the word *Bundschuh*, the worthy painter gave a start, and swore that not for the wealth of the Holy Roman Empire itself would he undertake such a business. They all saw that it was no use pressing him any further, and so contented themselves with threatening him with dire consequences should he divulge the conversation that he had had with them. Hans Enderlin also reminded him that he had already taken an oath of secrecy in all matters relating to the village, on his engagement to do church work, a circumstance that curiously enough illustrates the conditions of medieval life. The painter, fearful of not receiving his pay for the church work, if nothing worse, prudently kept silent.

Joss was at his wits' end. The silk of the flag was already bought, and even sewn; blue, with a white cross in the middle, were the colours; but to begin operations before the sign of the *Bundschuh* was painted, entered into the head of no one. In accordance with the current belief in magic, the symbol itself was supposed to possess a virtue, without the aid of which it was impossible to hope for success. There was nothing left for it but for Joss to start on a journey to the free city of Heilbronn in Swabia, where he knew there lived a painter of some ability. Arrived there, Joss dissembled his real object, pretending that he was a Swiss, who, when fighting in a great battle, had made a vow that if he came out safe and sound, he would undertake a pilgrimage to Aachen (Aix-la-Chapelle), and there dedicate a banner to the mother of God. He begged the painter to make a suitable design for him, with a crucifix, the Virgin and St. John the Baptist, and underneath a *Bundschuh*. The Heilbronn artist was staggered at the latter suggestion, and asked what he meant. Joss appeared quite innocent, and said that he was a shoemaker's son from Stein-am-Rhein, that his father had a *Bundschuh* as his trade-sign, and in order that it might be known that the gift was from him, he wished his family emblem to appear upon it. Round the flag were to be the words: "Lord, defend Thy Divine justice". These representations overcame the painter's scruples, and in a few days the banner was finished. Hiding it under his doublet, Joss hurried back to Lehen.

At last all was ready for the great coup. The *Kirchweihe* (or village festival, held every year on the name-day of the patron saint of a village church) wars being held at a neighbouring village on the 19th of October. This vas the date fixed for a final general meeting of the conspirators to determine the plan of attack and to decide whether Freiburg should be its object, or some smaller town in the neighbourhood. The confederates in Elsass were ordered, as soon as the standard of revolt was raised in Breisgau (Baden), to move across the Rhine to Burkheim, where the banner of the league would be flying. Special instructions were given to the beggars to spy round the towns and in all inns and alehouses, and to bring reports to Lehen. Arrangements were also made for securing at least one or two adherents in each of the guilds in Freiburg. All these orders were carried out in accordance with the directions made by Joss before his departure. But whilst he was away the members lost their heads. When too late they bethought themselves to win over an old experienced warrior who lived in Freiburg, a cousin of one of the chief conspirators at Lehen. Had they done so earlier it is likely enough that he would have been able to secure them possession of the city. As it happened, things were managed too hurriedly. Before matters were ripe the chief men grew careless of all precautions, so confident were they of success. One of the conspirators within the city set fire to a stable with a view to creating a panic, in the course of which the keys of the city gates might be stolen and the leaguers admitted. The attempt, however, was discovered before the fire gained any hold, and merely put the authorities on the alert. Again, three members of the league seized upon a peasant a short distance from the city, dragged him into a neighbouring wood, and made him swear allegiance. After he had done this under compulsion they exposed to him their intentions as to Freiburg. The peasant proving recalcitrant, even to the extent of expressing horror at the proposal, the three drew their knives upon him, and would have murdered him when the sound of horses vas heard on the high road close by, and, struck with panic, they let him go and hid themselves in the recesses of the wood. The peasant, of course, revealed all to his confessor the same evening, and wanted to know whether the oath he had taken under compulsion was binding on him. The priest put himself at once in communication with the Imperial Comirilssatry of Freiburg, who made the City Corporation acquainted with the facts. Two other traitors a few days after came to the assistance of the authorities, and revealed many important secrets. Count Philip of Baden, their over-lord, to whom these disclosures were made, was not long in placing them at the disposal of the Corporation of Freiburg and of the Austrian Government at Ensisheim. Late the following night, October 4, messengers were sent in all directions to warn the authorities of the neighbouring villages and towns to prepare themselves for the outbreak of the conspiracy. Double watches were placed at the gates of Freiburg and on all the towers of the walls. The guilds were called together, and their members instructed to wake each other up immediately , on the sound of the storm-bell, when they were all to meet in the cathedral close. The moment that these preparations were known at Lehen, a meeting was called together on the *Hardmatte* at vespers; but in the absence of Joss Fritz, and, as ill-luck would have it, in that also of one or two of the best organisers who were away on business of the league, divided counsels prevailed. In the very midst of all this, two hundred citizens of Freiburg armed to the teeth appeared in Lehen, seized Huns Enderlin and his son, as also Elsa, the woman with whom Joss had been living besides other leading men of the movement. Panic now reigned amongst all concerned. Well nigh every one took to flight, most of them succeeding in crossing the frontier to Switzerland. The news of the collapse of the movement apparently reached Joss before he arrived in Lehen, as there is no evidence of his having returned there. Many of the conspirators met together in Basel, amongst them being Joss Fritz with his banner. They decided to seek an asylum in Zurich. But they were fallen upon on the way, and two were made prisoners, the rest, among them Joss, escaping. Those of the conspirators who were taken prisoners behaved heroically; not the most severe tortures could induce them to reveal anything of importance. As a consequence, comparatively few of those compromised fell victims to the vengeance of their noble and clerical enemies. In Elsass they were not so fortunate as in Baden, many persons being executed on suspicion. The Imperial Councillor Rudolph was even sent into Switzerlancl to demand the surrender of the fugitives, and two were given up by Schaffhausen. Joss's mistress was liberated after three weeks, and she was suspected of having harboured him at different times afterwards. The last distinct traces of him are to be found in the Black Forest ten years later, during the great rising; but they are slight, and merely indicate his having taken a part in this movement. Thus this interesting personality disappears from human ken. Did the energetic and enthusiastic peasant leader fall a victim to noble vengeance in 1525, or did he withdraw from public life to a tranquil old age in some obscure village of Southern Germany? These are questions which we shall now, it is probable, never be able to answer.

At the same time that the foregoing events were taking place there was a considerable ferment in Switzerland. Increase of luxury was beginning to tell there also. The simple cloth or

51

sheepskin of the old *Eidgenosse* was now frequently replaced, in the towns especially, by French and Italian dresses, by doublets of scarlet silk, by ostrich feathers, and even by cloth of gold. In the cities domestic architecture began to take on the sumptuousness of the Renaissance style. The coquettish alliance with Louis XI. in the preceding century had already opened a way for the introduction of French customs. Gambling for high stakes became the fashionable amusement in town and country alike. The story of Hans Waldmann, although belonging to a period some years earlier than that of this history, illustrates a decline from the primitive simplicity of the ancient Switzer, a decline which had become infinitely more accentuated and general at the time of which we treat. All this led, of course, to harder conditions for the peasants, which, in the summer of 1513, issued in several minor revolts. In some cases, notably in that of the peasants of Canton Bern, the issue was favourable to the insurgents.

In the neighbouring country of Würtemberg an insurrection also burst forth. It is supposed to have had some connection with the *Bundschuh* movement at Lehen; but it took the name of "The Poor Conrad". It was immediately occasioned by the oppression of Duke Ulrich of Würtemberg, who, to cover the expenses of his luxurious court, was burdening the peasants with ever-fresh exactions. He had already made debts to the extent of a million golden. The towns, no less than the peasantry, were indignant at the rapacity and insolence of the minions of this potentate. First, an income-tax was imposed without the concurrence of the estates, which should have been consulted. Next, an impost was laid on the daily consumption of meal and wine. The butchers and millers and vintners were then allowed to falsify their weights and measures, on the condition that the greater part of their increased profits went to the duke. "The Poor Conrad" demanded the removal of all these abuses; and, in addition, the freedom of the chase, of fishery and of wood-cutting, and the abolition of villein service. In the towns the poorer citizens, including both guildsmen and journeymen, were prepared to seize the opportunity of getting rid of their *Ebarkeit*. This movement was also, like the *Bundschuh* at Lehen, suppressed for the time being. We leave gone at length into the history of the *Bundschuh* as a type of the manner in which the peasant movements of the time were planned and organised. The methods pursued by "The Poor Conrad," the midnight meetings, the secret pass-words, the preparations for sudden risings, were in most respects similar. The skilled and well-equipped knighthood of Dune Ulrich, though inferior in numbers, readily dispersed the ill-armed and inexperienced bands of peasants whom they encountered. To this result the treacherous promises of Duke Ulrich, which induced large numbers of peasants to lay down their arms, contributed. The revolt proved a flash in the pan; and although those who had partaken in it were not punished with the merciless severity shown by the Austrian Government at Ensisheim, it yet resulted in no amelioration of the conditions of the people. Many of the leaders, and not a few of the rank and file, fled the country, and, as in the case of the Lehen *Bundschuh*, found a refuge in Northern Switzerland.

In the autumn of 1517 Baden was once more the scene of an attempted peasant rising, its objects being again much the same as were those of the previous enterprises. Rent and interest were to be abolished, and no lord recognised except the Emperor. The plan was to surprise and capture the towns of Weissenburg and Hagenau, and to make a clean sweep of the imperial councillors and judges, as well as of the knights and nobles. This conspiracy was, however, also discovered before the time for action was ripe. There were also, in various parts of Central Europe, other minor attempts at revolt and conspiracies which it is not necessary to particularise here. The great rebellion of the year 1514, in Hungary, however, although not strictly coming within the limits of our subject, deserves a few words of notice.

At Easter, in that year, the whole of Hungary was stirred up by the preaching of a crusade against the Turks, then hard pressing the eastern frontier. All who joined the crusade, down to the lowest serf, were promised not merely absolution, but freedom. The movement was immensely popular, thousands crowding to the standards. The nobles naturally viewed the movement with disfavour; many, in fact, sallied forth from their castles with their retinues to fetch back the fugitives. In many cases the seizures were accompanied with every circumstance of cruelty. As the news of these events reached the assembled bands in their camp, a change of disposition became manifest. The enthusiasm for vanquishing the Turk abroad speedily gave way to an enthusiasm for vanquishing the Turk at home. Everywhere throughout the camp were heard threats of vengeance. Finally, one George Dozes, who would seem to have been a genuine popular hero in the best sense of the word, placed himself at their head. George Doza's aims were not confined to mere vengeance on the offending nobles. They extended to the conception of a complete reorganisation of the conditions of the oppressed classes throughout the country. In vain an order came from the Court at Ofen for the army to disperse. Dozes divided his forces into five bodies, each of which was to concentrate its efforts on a definite district, at the same time summoning the whole population to join. The destruction of castles, and the slaughter of their inmates, became general throughout the land. For a moment the nobles seemed paralysed; but they soon recovered themselves, and two of their number, Johann Zapolya and Johann Boremiszsza, aided by the inhabitants of the city of Buda-Pesth, got together as array to save the situation for their colleagues. They were not long in joining battle with the insurgents. The latter, deserted at the beginning by some of their leaders, who went over to the enemy, fought bravely, but had eventually to yield to superior arms and discipline. A large number of prisoners were taken, of whom the majority were barbarously executed, and the rest sent home, with ears and noses cut off.

Meanwhile, George Doza, who had been besieging Szegedin, withdrew his forces, and gave battle to Bishop Csaky and the Count of Temeswar, who were advancing with troops to relieve the town. After two days' hard fighting, victory rewarded the bravery of the peasants. Doza's followers demanded vengeance for their murdered and mutilated comrades. The bishop was impaled, and the royal treasurer of the district hanged on a high gallows. But Doza's was the only division of the popular army that met with any success. The rest, on coming to grips with the nobles, were dispersed and almost annihilated. The remnants joined the forces of their commander-in -chief, whose army was thus augmented from day to day. Doza now issued a decree abolishing king and higher and lower nobility, deposing all bishops save one, and proclaiming the equality of all men before God. One of his lieutenants then succeeded in recruiting what amounted to a second army, containing a large force of cavalry. He moved on Temeswar, but committed the imprudence of undertaking a long siege of this powerful fortress. After two months his army began to get demoralised. A few days before the place would have had to surrender, Doza was surprised by the Transylvanian Army. In spite of this, however, he deployed his troops with incredible rapidity, and a terrific battle, long undecided, ensued. After several hours of hard fighting, one of the wings of Doza's army took to flight. General confusion followed, in the midst of which Doza might have been seen in the forefront of the battle like an ancient hero, hewing down nobles right and left, until his sword broke in his hind. He was then instantly seized, and made prisoner in company with his brother Gregory. The latter was imediately beheaded. Doza and about forty of his officers were thrown into a vile dungeon in Temeswar and deprived of all nourishment. On the fourteenth day of their incarceration, nine alone remained alive. These nine, Doza at their head, were led out into the open space before their prison. All iron throne was erected there and made red hot, and Doza, loaded with chains, was forcibly placed upon it. A red-hot iropn crown was laid upon his head, and a red-hot iron sceptre thrust into his hand. His companions were then offered their lives on condition that they forthwith tore off and devoured the flesh of their leader. Three, who refused with indignation, were at once hewn in pieces. Six did as they were bidden. "Dogs!" cried Doza. This was the only sound that escaped him. Torn with red-hot iron pincers, he died. The defeated peasants were impaled and hanged by the hundred. It is estimated that over 60,000 of them perished in this war, and in the reprisals that followed it. The result of the insurrection was a more brutal oppression than had ever been known before.

At the same time various insurrections of a local nature were taking place in Germany and in the Austrian territories. Amid the Styrian and Carinthian Alps there were movements of the peasants, who, in these remote mountain districts, seem to have retained more of their primitive independence. In the south-west of Austria there were three duchies — Kärnthen (Carinthia), Steuermarck (Styria), and the Krain. At Kärnburg, a short distance from Klagenfurt, was a round stone, on which were engraved the arms of the country. When a duke assumed the sovereignty, a peasant belonging to one of the ancient families of a neighbouring village in which this particular right was hereditary, attended to offer the new duke the homage of the peasantry. Round the stone, on which sat the aged representative of the rural communities, the peasantry of the neighbourhood were gathered. The over-lord, attired in peasantly costume, advanced towards the stone. With him were two local dignitaries, one leading a lean black cow, the other an underfed horse. Bringing up the rear followed the remaining nobility and knighthood, with the banner of the duchy. The peasant who was sitting on the fateful stone cried: "Who is he who advances so proudly into our country?" The surrounding peasants answered: "It is our prince who comes". "Is he a righteous judge?" asked the peasant on the stone. "Will he promote the well-being of our land and its freedom. Is he a protector of the Christian faith and of widows and orphans?" The multitude shouted: "This he is, and will ever be so". That part of the ceremony concluded, the duke had to take an oath to the peasant on the stone that he would not disdain, for the welfare of the land, in any of the respects mentioned, to nourish himself with such a wretched beast as the cow accompanying him, or to ride on such a lean and ill-favoured steed. The peasant on the stone then gave the duke a light box on the cars, and conjured him in patriarchal fashion to remain ever a righteous judge and a father to his people. The old countryman then stood up, and the nobles surrendered to him the cow and horse, which he led home as his property.

The above singular custom had been kept up in Carinthia until the middle of the fifteenth century, when the Emperor Frederick III refused, in his capacity of local lord, to don the peasant garb, although he compromised the matter by giving the peasants a deed establishing them in their ancient freedom. The growing pressure of taxation and the new imposts, which the wars of Maximilian entailed, led, at the beginning of the sixteenth century, to an agitation here also, and, finally, to a rising in which, it is said, as many as 90,000 peasants took part, but which did not immediately come to a head, owing to timely concessions on the hart of the Emperor. The league of the peasants, in this case, extended over Styria as well as Carinthia and the Krain. It broke forth again in the spring of 1517 owing to renewed oppressions on the part of the nobles. Several castles, during the three months that the revolt lasted, were destroyed, and large stretches of country laid waste. Not a few nobles were hurled from their own turrets. The Emperor Maximilian, who, throughout the whole affair, showed himself not unfavourable to the cause of the peasants, held his hand, as it would seem, so long as the latter confined themselves to punishing the notoriously rapacious among the territorial magnates; but afterwards, when the armed bodies of peasants gradually melted away, and those that remained lost all discipline, degenerating into mere plundering bands, he sent a party of a few hundred knights, who speedily routed the ill-armed and disorderly horde's. Little quarter was given to the fugitives, and the usual bloody executions followed. There was, in addition, a heavy indemnity laid on the whole peasantry, which took the form of a perpetual tax. The revolt in the Krain lasted longest, and was suppressed with the most bloodshed. Those in Styria and Carinthia came to an end much sooner, and with less disastrous results to those who had been engaged in them.

But it was not alone in Germany, or, indeed, in Central Europe, that a general stirring was visible among the peasant populations at the beginning of the sixteenth century. It is true that the great revolts, the Wat Tyler insurrection in England, and the Jacquerie in France, took place long before; but even when there was no great movement, sporadic excitement was everywhere noticeable. In Spain, we read of a peasant revolt, which Cornelius Agrippa of Nettesheim was engaged by the territorial lord to quell by his supposed magical powers. In England, the disturbances of Henry VIII.'s reign, connected with the suppression of the monasteries, are well known. The expropriation of the people from the soil to make room for sheep-farms also gave occasion to periodical disturbances of a local character, which culminated in 1549 in the famous revolt led by John Ket in East Anglia.

The deep-reaching importance and effective spread of movements was infinitely greater in the Middle Ages than in modern times. The same phenomenon presents itself to-day in barbaric and semi-barbaric communities. At first sight one is inclined to think that there has been no period in the world's history when it was so easy to stir up a population as the present, with our newspapers, our telegraphs, our postal arrangements and our railways. But this is just one of those superficial notions that are not confirmed by history. We are similarly apt to think that there was no age in which travel was so widespread, and formed so great a part of the education of mankind as at present. There could be no greater mistake. The true age of travelling was the close of the Middle Ages, or what is known as the Renaissance period. The man of learning, then just differentiated from the ecclesiastic, spent the greater part of his life in carrying his intellectual wares from court to court, and from university to university, just as the merchant personally carried his goods from city to city in an age in which commercial correspondence, bill-brokers, and the varied forms of modern business were but in embryo. It was then that travel really meant education, the acquirement of thorough and intimate knowledge of diverse manners and customs. Travel was then not then pastime, but a serious element in life.

In the same way the spread of a political or social movement was at least as rapid then as now, and far more penetrating. The methods were, of course, vastly different from the present; but the human material to be dealt with was far easier to mould, and kept its shape much more readily when moulded, than is the case now-a-days. The appearance of a religious or political teacher in a village or small town of the Middle Ages was an event which keenly excited the interest of the inhabitants. It struck across the path of their daily life, leaving behind it a track hardly conceivable to-day. For one of the salient symptoms of the change which has taken place since that time is the disappearance of local centres of activity, and the transference of the intensity of life to a few large towns. In the Middle Ages, every town, small no less than large, was a more or less self-sufficing organism, intellectually and industrially, and was not essentially dependent on the outside world for its social sustenance. This was especially the case in Central Europe, where communication was much more imperfect and dangerous than in Italy, France, or England. In a society without newspapers, without easy communication with the rest of the world, when the vast majority could neither read nor write, when books were rare and costly, and accessible only to the privileged few, a new idea bursting upon one of these communities was eagerly welcomed, discussed in the council chamber of the town, in the hall of the castle, in the refectory of the monastery, at the social board of the burgess, in the workroom, and, did it but touch his interests, in the hut of the peasant. It was canvassed, too, at church festivals

(*Kirchweihe*), the only regular occasion on which the inhabitants of various localities came together. In the absence of all other distraction, men thought it out in all the bearings which their limited intellectual horizon permitted. If calculated in any way to appeal to them, it soon struck root, and became a part of their very nature, a matter for which, if occasion were, they were prepared to sacrifice goods, liberty, and even life itself. In the present day a new idea is comparative) slow in taking root. Amid the myriad distractions of modern life, perpetually chasing one another, there is no time for any one thought, however wide-reaching in its bearings, to take a firm hold. In order that it should do this in the *modern mind,* it must be again and again borne in upon this, not always too receptive intellectual substance. People require to read of it day after day in their newspapers, or to hear it preached from countless platforms, before any serious effect is created. In the simple life of former ages it was not so.

The mode of transmitting intelligence, especially such as was connected with the stirring up of political and religious movements, was in those days of a nature of which we have now little conception. The sort of thing in vogue then may be compared to the methods adopted in India to prepare the mutiny of 1857, when the mysterious cake was passed from village to village, signifying that the moment had come for the outbreak. We have already seen how Joss Fritz used the guild of beggars as fetchers and carriers of news and as auxiliaries in his organisation generally. The fact is noteworthy, moreover, that his confidence in them does not seem to have been misplaced, for the collapse of the movement cannot certainly he laid to their account. The sense of *esprit de corps* and of that kind of honour most intimately associated with it is, it must also be remembered, infinitely keener in ruder states of society than under a high civilisation. The growth of civilisation, as implying the disruption of the groups in which the individual is merged under more primitive conditions, and his isolation as an autonomous unit having vague and very elastic moral duties to his "country" or to the whole of mankind, but none towards any definite and proximate social whole, necessarily destroys that communal spirit which prevails in the former case. This is one of the striking truths which the history of these peasant risings illustrates in various ways and brings vividly home to us.

Footnotes

1. We adopt the German spelling of the name of the province usually known in this country as Alsace, for the reason that at the time of which this history treats it had never been French; and the French language was probably little more known there than in other parts of Germany.

2. It will he seen from the historical map that Breisgau and Sundgau were feudal appanages of the house of Austria. Ensisheim was the scat of the *Habsburg* overlordship in the district (not to he confounded with the *imperial* power).

II. The Reformation Movement

The "great man" theory of history, formerly everywhere prevalent, and even now common among non-historical persons, has long regarded the Reformation as the purely personal work of the Augustine monk who was its central figure. The fallacy of this conception is particularly striking in the case of the Reformation. Not only was it preceded by numerous sporadic outbursts of religious revivalism which sometimes took the shape of opposition to the dominant form of Christianity, though it is true they generally shaded off into mere movements of independent Catholicism within the Church; but there were in addition |at least two distinct religions movements which led up to it, while much which, under the reformers of the sixteenth century, appears as a distinct and separate theology, is traceable in the fourteenth and fifteenth centuries in the mystical movement connected with the names of Meister Eckhart and Tauler. Meister Echhart, whose free treatment of Christian doctrines, in order to bring them into consonance with his mystical theology, had drawn him into conflict with the Papacy, undoubtedly influenced Luther through his disciple, Tauler, and especially through the book which proceeded from the latter's school, the *Deutsche Theologie*. It is, however, in the much more important movement, which originated with Wyclif and extended to Central Europe through Huss, that we must look for the more obvious influences determining the course of religious development in Germany.

The Wyclitfite movement in England was less a doctrinal heterodoxy than a revolt against the Papacy and the priestly hierarchy. Mere theoretical speculations were seldom interfered with, but anything which touched their material interests at once aroused the vigilance of the clergy. It is noticeable that the diffusion of Lollardism, that is of the ideas of Wyclif, if not the cause of, was at least followed by the peasant rising under the leadership of John Ball, a connection which is also visible in the Tziska revolt following the Hussite movement, and the Peasants' War in Germany which came on the heels of the Lutheran, Reformation. How much Huss was directly influenced by the teachings of Wyclif is clear. The works of the latter were widely circulated throughout Europe; for one of the advantages of the custom of writing in Latin, which was universal during the Middle Ages, was that books of an important character were immediately current amongst all scholars without having, as now, to wait upon the caprice and ability of translators. Huss read Wyclif's works as the preparation for his theological degree, and subsequently made them his text-books when teaching at the University of Prague. After his treacherous execution at Constance, and the events which followed thereupon In Bohemia, a number of Hussite fugitives settled in Southern Germany, carrying with them the seeds of the new doctrines. An anonymous contemporary writer states that "to John Huss and his followers are to be traced almost all those false principles concerning the power of the spiritual and temporal authorities and the possession of earthly goods and rights which before in Bohemia, and now with us, have called forth revolt and rebellion, plunder, arson, and murder, and have shaken to its foundations the whole commonwealth. The poison of these false doctrines has been long flowing from Bohemia into Germany, and will produce the same desolating consequences wherever it spreads."

The condition of the Catholic Church, against which the Reformation movement generally was a protest, needs here to be made clear to the reader. The beginning of clerical disintegration is distinctly visible in the first half of the fourteenth century. The interdicts, as an institution, had ceased to be respected, and the priesthood itself began openly to sink itself in debauchery and to play fast and loose with the rites of the Church. Indulgences for a hundred years were readily granted for a consideration. The manufacture of relics became an organised branch of industry; and festivals of fools and festivals of asses were invented by the jovial priests themselves in travesty of sacred mysteries, as a welcome relaxation from the monotony of prescribed ecclesiastical ceremony. Pilgrimages increased in number and frequency; new saints were created by the dozen; and the disbelief of the clergy in the doctrines they professed was manifest even to the most illiterate, whilst contempt for the ceremonies they practised was openly displayed in the performance of their clerical functions. An illustration of this is the joke of the priests related by Luther, who were wont during the celebration of the mass, when the worshippers fondly imagined that the sacred formal of transubstantiaton was being repeated, to replace the words *Panis es et carnem fiebis*, "Bread than art and flesh thou shall become," by *Panis es et panem manibus*, "Bread than art and bread than shall remain".

The scandals as regards clerical manners, growing, as they had been, for many generations, reached their climax in the early part of the sixteenth century. It was a common thing for priests to drive a roaring trade as moneylenders, landlords of alehouses and gambling dens, and, even in some cases, brothel-keepers. Papal ukases had proved ineffective to stem the current of clerical abuses. The regular clergy evoked even more indignation than the secular. "Stinking cowls" was a favourite epithet for the monks. Begging, cheating, shameless ignorance, drunkeness and debauchery, are alleged as being their noted characteristics. One of the princes of the Empire addresses a prior of a convent largely patronised by aristocratic ladies as "Thou, our common brother-in-law!" In some of the convents of Friesland, promiscuous intercourse between the sexes was, it is said, quite openly practised, the offspring being reared as monks and nuns. The different orders competed with each other for the fame and wealth to be obtained out of the public credulity. A fraud attempted by the Dominicans at Bern, in 1506, *with the concurrence of the heads of the order throughout Germany*, was one of the main causes of that city adopting the Reformation.[1]

In addition to the increasing burdens of investitures,

annates, and other Papal dues, the brunt of which the German people had directly or indirectly to bear, special offence was given at the beginning of the sixteenth century by the excessive exploitation of the practice of indulgences by Leo X. for the purpose of completing the cathedral of St. Peter's at Rome. It was this, coming on the top of the exactions already rendered necessary by the increasing luxury and debauchery of the Papal Court and those of the other ecclesiastical dignitaries, that directly led to the dramatic incidents with which the Lutheran Reformation opened.

The remarkable personality with which the religious side of the Reformation is pre-eminently associated was a child of his time, who had passed through a variety of mental struggles, and had already broken through the bonds of the old ecclesiasticism before that turning point in his career which is usually reckoned the opening of the Reformation, to wit — the nailing of the theses on to the door of the Schloss-Kirche in Wittenberg on the 31st of October, 1517. Martin Luther, we must always bear in mind, however, was no Protestant in the English Puritan sense of the word. It was not merely that he retained much of what would be deemed by the old-fashioned English Protestant "Romish error" in his doctrine, but his practical view of life showed a reaction from the ascetic pretensions which he had seen bred nothing but hypocrisy and the worst forms of sensual excess. It is, indeed, doubtful if the man who sang the praises of " Wine, Women, and Song " would have been deemed a fit representative in Parliament or elsewhere by the British Nonconformist conscience of our day; or would he acceptable in any capacity to the grocer-deacon of our provincial towns, who, not content with being allowed to sand his sugar and adulterate his tea unrebuked, would socially ostracise every one whose conduct did not square with his conventional shibboleths. Martin Luther was a child of his time also as a boon companion. The freedom of his living in the years following his rupture with Rome was the subject of severe animadversions on the part of the noble, but in this respect narrow-minded Thomas Münzer, who in his open letter addressed to the "Soft-living flesh of Wittenberg," scathingly denounces what he deems his debauchery. It does not enter into our province here to discuss at length the religious aspects of the Reformation; but it is interesting to note in passing, the more than modern liberality of Luther's views with respect to the marriage question and the celibacy of the clergy, contrasted with the strong Medieval flavour of his belief in witchcraft and sorcery. In his *De Captivate Babylonica Ecclesiae* (1519) he expresses the view that if, for any cause, husband or wife are prevented from having sexual intercourse they are justified, the woman equally with the man, in seeking it elsewhere. He was opposed to divorce, though he did not forbid it, and recommended that a man should rather have a plurality of wives than that he should put away any one of them. Luther held strenuously the view that marriage was a purely external contract for the purpose of sexual satisfaction, and in no way entered into the spiritual life of the man. On this ground he sees no objection in the so-called mixed marriages, which were, of course, frowned upon by the Catholic Church. In his sermon on "Married Life" he says: "Know therefore that marriage is an outward thing, like any other worldly business. Just as I may eat, drink, sleep, walk, ride, buy, speak and bargain with a heathen, a Jew, a Turk or a heretic; so may I also be and remain married to such an one, and I care not one jot for the fool's laws which forbid it ..... A heathen is just as much man or woman, well and shapely made by God, as St. Peter, St. Paul, or St. Lucia." Nor did he shrink from applying his views to particular cases, as is instanced by his correspondence with Philip von Hesse, whose constitution appears to have required more than one wife. He here lays down explicitly the doctrine that polygamy and concubinage are not forbidden to Christians, though, in his advice to Philip, he adds the *caveat* that he should keep the matter dark to the end that offence might not be given; "for," says he, "it matters not, provided one's conscience is right, what others say". In one of his sermons on the Pentateuch[2] we find the words: "It is not forbidden that a man have more than one wife. I would not forbid it to-day, albeit I would not advise it .... Yet neither would I condemn it." Other opinions on the nature of the sexual relations were equally broad; for in one of his writings on monastic celibacy his words plainly indicate his belief that chastity, no more than other fleshly mortifications, was to be considered a divine ordinance for all men or women. In an address to the clergy he says: "A woman not possessed of high and rare grace call no more abstain from a man than from eating, drinking, sleeping, or other natural function. Likewise a man cannot abstain from a woman. The reason is that it is as deeply implanted in our nature to breed children as it is to eat and drink."[3] The worthy Janssen observes in a scandalised tone that Luther, as regards certain matters relating to married life, "gave expression to principles before unheard of in Christian Europe;"[4] and the British Nonconformist of to-day, if he reads these "immoral" opinions of the hero of the Reformation, will be disposed to echo the sentiments of the Ultramontane historian.

The relation of the Reformation to the "New Learning" was in Germany not unlike that which existed in the other northern countries of Europe, and notably in England. Whilst the hostility of the latter to the mediaeval Church was very marked, and it was hence disposed to regard the religious Reformation as an ally, this had not proceeded very far before the tendency of the Renaissance spirit was to side with Catholicism against the new theology and dogma, as merely destructive and hostile to culture. The men of the Humanist movement were for the most part Freethinkers, and it was with them that freethought first appeared in modern Europe. They therefore had little sympathy with the narrow bigotry of religious reformers, and preferred to remain in touch with the Church, whose then loose and tolerant Catholicism have freer play to intellectual speculations, provided they steered clear of overt theological heterodoxy, than the newer systems, which, taking theology *au grand sérieux*, tended to regard profane art and learning as more or less superfluous, and spent their whole time in theological wrangles. Nevertheless, there were not wanting men who, influenced at first by the revival of learning, ended by throwing themselves entirely Into the Reformation movement, though in these cases they were usually actuated rather by their hatred of the Catholic hierarchy than by any positive religious sentiment.

Of such men Ulrich von Hutten, the descendent of an ancient and influential knightly family, was a noteworthy example. After having already acquired fame us the author of a series of skits in the new Latin, and other works of classical scholarship, being also well known as the ardent supporter of Reuchlin in his dispute with the Church, and as the friend and correspondent of the Central Humanist figure of the time, Erasmus, he watched with absorbing interest the movement which Luther had inaugurated. Six months after the nailing of the theses at Wittenherg, he writes enthusiastically to a friend respecting the growing ferment in ecclesiastical matters, evidently regarding, the new movement as a Kilkenny-cat fight. "The leaders," he says, "are bold and hot, full of courage and zeal. Now they shout and cheer, now they lament and bewail, as loud as they can. They have lately set themselves to write; the printers are getting enough to do. Propositions, corollaries, conclusions, and articles are being sold. For this alone I hope they will mutually destroy each other." "A few months ago a monk was telling me what was going on in Saxony, to which I replied: 'Devour each other in order that ye in turn may be devoured (sic)'. Pray Heaven that our enemies may fight each other to the bitter end, and by their obstinacy extinguish each other." From this it will he seen that Hutten regarded the Reformation in its earlier stages as merely a monkish squabble, and failed to see the tremendous upheaval of all the old landmarks of ecclesiastical domination which was immanent in it. So soon, however as he perceived its real significance, he threw himself wholly into the movement. It must not be forgotten, moreover, that, although Hutten's zeal for Humanism made him welcome any attempt to overthrow the power of the clergy and the monks, he had also an eminently political motive for his action in what was, in some respects, the main object of his life, *viz.*, to rescue the "knighthood," or smaller nobility, from having their independence crushed out by the growing powers of the princes of the Empire. Probably more than one-third of the manors were held by ecclesiastical dignitaries, so that anything which threatened their possessions and privileges seemed to strike a blow at the very foundations of the imperial system. Hutten hoped that the new doctrines would set the princes by the ears all round; and that then, by allying themselves with the reforming party, the knighthood might succeed in retaining the privileges which still remained to them, but were rapidly slipping away, and might even regain some of those which had been already lost. It was not till later, however, that Hutten saw matters in this light. He was at the time the above letter was written in the service of the Archbishop Albrecht of Mainz, the leading favourer of the new learning amongst the prince-prelates, and it was mainly from the Humanist standpoint that he regarded the beginnings of the Reformation. After leaving the service of the archbishop he struck up a personal friendship with Luthor, instigated thereto by his political chief, Franz von Sickingen, the leader of the knighthood, from whom he probably received the first intimation of the importance of the new movement to their common cause.

When in 1520 the young Emperor, Charles V., was crowned at Aachen, Luther's party, as well as the knighthood, expected that considerable changes would result in a sense favourable to their position from the presumed pliability of the new head of the Empire. His youth, it was supposed, would make him more sympathetic to the newer spirit which was rapidly developing itself; and it is true that about the time of his election Charles lead shown a transient favour to the "recalcitrant monk". It would appear, however, that this was only for the purpose of frightening the Pope into abandoning his declared intention of abolishing the Inquisition in Spain, then regarded as one of the mainstays of the royal power, and still more to exercise pressure upon him, in order that he should facilitate Charles's designs on the Milanese territory. Once these objects were attained, he was just as ready to oblige the Pope by suppressing the new anti-Papal movement as he might possibly otherwise have been to have favoured it with a view to humbling the only serious rival to his dominion in the Empire.

Immediately after his coronation, he proceeded to Cologne and convoked by imperial edict a Reichstag at Worms for the following 27th of January, 1521. The proceedings of this famous Reichstag have been unfortunately so identified with the edict against Luther that the other important matters which were there discussed have almost fallen into oblivion. At least two other questions were dealt with, however, which are significant of the changes that were then taking place. The first was the rehabilitation and strengthening of the Imperial Governing Council (*Reichs-Regiment*), whose functions under Maximilian had been little more than nominal. There was at first a feeling amongst the States in favour of transferring all authority to it, even during the residence of the Emperor in the Empire; and in the end, while having granted to it complete power during his absence, it practically retained very much of this power when he was present. In constitution it was very similar to the French "Parliaments," and like them was principally composed of learned jurists, four being elected by the Emperor and the remainder by the estates. The character and the great powers of this council, extending even to ecclesiastical matters during the ensuing years, undoubtedly did much to hasten on the substitution of the civil law for the older customary or common law, a matter which we shall consider more in detail later on. The financial condition of the Empire was also considered; and it here first became evident that the dislocation of economic conditions, which had begun with the century, would render an enormously increased taxation necessary to maintain the imperial authority, amounting to five times as much as had previously been required.

It was only after these secular affairs of the Empire had been disposed of that the deliberations of the Reichstag on ecclesiastical matters were opened by the indictment of Luther in a long speech by Aleander, one of the papal nuncios, in introducing the Pope's letter. In spite of the efforts of his friends, Luther was not permitted to be present at the beginning of the proceedings; but subsequently he was sent for by the Emperor, in order that he might state his case. His journey to Worms was one long triumph, especially at Erfurt, where he was received with enthusiasm by the Humanists as the enemy of the Papacy. But his presence in the Reichstag was unavailing, and the proceedings resulted in his being placed under the ban of the Empire. The safe-conduct of the Emperor was, however, in his case respected; and in spite of the fears of his friends that a like fate might befall him as had befallen Huss after the Council of Constance, he was allowed to depart unmolested.

On his way to Wittenberg Luther was seized by arrangement with his supporter, the Kurfürst of Saxony, and conveyed in safety to the Castle of Wartburg, in Thuringen, a report in the meantime being industriously circulated by certain of his adherents, with a view of arousing popular feeling, that he had been arrested by order of the Emperor and was being tortured. In this way he was secured from all danger for the time being, and it was during his subsequent stay that he laid the foundations of the literary language of Germany.

Says a contemporary writer,[5] an eye-witness of what went on at Worms during the sitting of the Reichstag: "all is disorder and confusion. Seldom a night doth pass but that three or four persons be slain. The Emperor hath installed a provost, who hath drowned, hanged, and murdered over a hundred men." He proceeds: "Stabbing, whoring, flesh-eating (it was in Lent .... altogether there is an orgie worthy of the Venusberg". He further states that many gentlemen and other visitors had drunk themselves to death on the strong Rhenish wine. Aleander was in danger of being murdered by the Lutheran populace, instigated thereto by Hutten's inflammatory letters from the neighbouring Castle of Ebernburg, in which Franz yon Sichingen had given him a refuge. The fiery Humanist wrote to Aleander himself, saying that he: would leave no stone unturned "till thou who camest hither full of wrath, madness, crime, and treachery shall be carried hence a lifeless corpse". Aleander naturally felt exceedingly uncomfortable, and other supporters of the Papal party were not less disturbed at the threats which seemed in a fair way of being carried out. The Emperor himself was without adequate means of withstanding a popular revolt should it occur. He had never been so low in cash or in men as at that moment. On the other hand, Sichingen, to whom he owed money, and who was the only man who could have saved the situation under the circumstances, had matters came to blows, was almost overtly on the side of the Lutherans; while the whole body of the impoverished knighthood were only awaiting a favourable opportunity to overthrow the power of the magnates, secular and ecclesiastic, with Sickingen as a leader. Such was the state of affairs at the beginning of the year 1521.

The ban placed upon Luther by the Reichstag marks the date of the complete rupture between the Reforming party and the old Church. Henceforward, many humanist and Humanistically influcnced persons who had supported him withdrew from the movement and swelled the ranks of the Conservatives. Foremost amongst these were Pirckheimer, the wealthy merchant and scholar of Nürnberg, and many others who dreaded lest the attack on ecclesiastical property and authority should, as indeed was the case, issue in a general attach on all property and authority. Thomas Murner, also, who was the type of the "moderate" of the situation, while professing to disapprove of the abuses of the Church, declared that Luther's manner of agitation could only lead to the destruction of all order, civil no less than ecclesiastical. The two parties were now clearly defined, and the points at issue were plainly irreconcilable with one another or involved irreconcilable details.

The printing press now for the first time appeared as the vehicle for popular literature; the art of the bard gave place to the art of the typographer, and the art of the preacher saw confronting it a formidable rival in that of the pamphleteer. Similarly in the French Revolution modern journalism, till then unimportant and sporadic, received its first great development, and began seriously to displace alike the preacher, the pamphlet, and the broadside. The flood of theological disquisitions, satires, dialogues, sermons, which now poured from every press in Germany, overflowed into all classes of society. These writings are so characteristic of the time that it is worth while devoting a few pages to their consideration, the more especially because it will afford us the opportunity for considering other changes in that spirit of the age, partly diseased growths of decaying mediaevalism, and partly the beginnings of the modern critical spirit, which also find expression in the literature of the Reformation period.

Footnotes

1. See Appendix 13 for this and an instance of a successful imposture.

2. *Sämmt. Werke*, xxxiii., 322-324.

3. Quoted in Janssen, *Ein Zweiter Wort an meine Kritiker*, 1883, p.94.

4. *Geschichte des Deutschen Volkes,* vol. ii., p.115.

5. Quoted in Janssen, bk. ii., 162.

III. Popular Literature of the Reformation

In accordance with the conventional view we have assumed in the preceding chapter that the Reichstag at Worms was a landmark in the history of the Reformation. This is, however, only true as regards the political side of the movement. The popular feeling was really quite continuous, at least from 1517 to 1525. With the latter year and the collapse of the peasant revolt a change is noticeable. In 1525, the Reformation as a great upstirring of the popular mind of Central Europe, in contradistinction to its character as an academic and purely political movement, reached high-water mark, and may almost be said to have exhausted itself. Until the latter year it was purely a revolutionary movement, attracting to itself all the disruptive elements of its time. Later, the reactionary possibilities within it declared themselves. The emancipation from the thraldom of the Catholic hierarchy and its Papal head, it was soon found, meant not emancipation from the arbitrary tyranny of the new political and centralising authorities then springing up, but, on the contrary, rather their consecration. The ultimate outcome, in fact, of the whole business was, as we shall see later on, the inculcation of the non-resistance theory as regards the civil power, and the clearing of the way for its extremest expression in the doctrine of the Divine Right of Kings, a theory utterly alien to the belief and practice of the Mediaeval Church.

The Reichstag of Worms, by cutting off all possibility of reconciliation, rather gave further edge to the popular revolutionary side of the movement than otherwise. The whole progress of the change in public feeling is plainly traceable in the mass of ephemeral literature that has come down to us from this period, broadsides, pamphlets, satires, folksongs, and the rest. The anonymous literature to which we more especially refer is distinguished by its coarse brutality and humour, even in the writings of the Reformers, which were themselves in no case remarkable for the suavity of their polemic.

Hutten, in some of his later vernacular poems, approaches the character of the less cultured broadside literature. To the critical mind it is somewhat amusing to note the enthusiasm with which the modern Dissenting and Puritan class contemplates the period of which we are writing, — an enthusiasm that would probably be effectively damped if the laudators of the Reformation knew the real character of the movement and of its principal actors.

The first attacks made by the broadside literature were naturally directed against the simony and benefice-gabbing of the clergy, a characteristic of the priestly office that has always powerfully appealed to the popular mind. Thus the "Courtisan and Benefice-eater" attacks the parasite of the Roman Court, who absorbs ecclesiastical revenues wholesale, putting in perfunctory *locum tenens* on the cheap, and begins:-

> I'm fairly called a Simonist and eke a Courtisan,
> And here to every peasant and every common man
> My knavery will very well appear.
> I called and cried to all who'd give me ear,
> To nobleman and knight and all above me
> "Behold me! And ye'll find I'll truly love ye."
> In another we read:-

The Paternoster teaches well

> How one for another his prayers should tell,
> Thro' brotherly love and not for gold,
> And good those same prayers God doth hold.
> So too with Holy Paul right clearly,
> Each shall his brother's load bear dearly.

But now, it declares, all that is changed. Now we are being taught just the opposite of God's teachings:-

> Such doctrine hath the priests increased,
> Whom men as masters now must feast,
> 'Fore all the crowd of Simonists,
> Whose waxing number no man wists,
> The towns and thorps seem full of them,
> And in all lands they're seen with shame.
> Their violence and knavery
> Leave not a church or living free.

A prose pamphlet, apparently published about the summer of 1520, shortly after Luther's excommunication, was the so-called "Wolf Song" (*Wolf-gesang*), which paints the enemies of Luther as wolves. It begins with a screed on the creation and fall of Adam, and a dissertation on the dogma of the Redemption; and then proceeds: "as one might say, dear brother, instruct me, for there; is now in our times so great commotion in faith come upon us. There is one in Saxony who is called Luther, of whom many pious and honest folk tell how that he doth write so consolingly the good evangelical (*evangelische*) truth. But again I hear that the Pope and the cardinals at Rome have but him under the ban as a heretic; and certain of our own preachers, too, scold him from their pulpits as a knave, a misleader, and a heretic. I am utterly confounded and know not where to turn; albeit my reason and heart do speak to me even as Luther writeth. But yet again it bethinks me that when the Pope, the cardinal, the bishop, the doctor, the monk and the priest, for the greater part are against him, and so that all save the common men and a few gentlemen, doctors, councillors and knights, are his adversaries, what shall I do?" "For answer, dear friend, get thee back and search the Scriptures, and thou shall find that so it hath gone with all the holy prophets even as it now fareth with Doctor Martin Luther, who is in truth a godly Christian and manly heart and only true Pope and apostle, when he the true office of the Apostles publicly fulfilleth..... If the *godly* man Luther were pleasing to the world, that were indeed a true sign that his doctrine were not from God the word of God is a fiery sword, that breaketh in pieces the rocks, and not a fox's tail or a reed that may be bent according to our pleasure." Seventeen noxious qualities of the wolf are adduced, his ravenousness, his cunning, his falseness, his cowardice, his thirst for robbery, amongst others. The Popes, the cardinals and the bishops are compared to the wolves in all their attributes: "The greater his pomp and splendour, the more shouldst thou beware of such an one; for he is a wolf that cometh in the shape of a good shepherd's dog. Beware! it is against the custom of Christ and His Apostles." It is again but the song of the wolves when they claim to mix themselves with worldly affairs and maintain the temporal supremacy. The greediness of the wolf is discernible in the means adopted to get money for the building of St. Peter's. The interlocutor is warned against giving to mendicant priests and monks. In this strain is the pamphlet continued, reference being made to Luther's dispute with Eck, who is sometimes called Dr. Gech, that is, Dr. Fop.

We have given this as a specimen of the almost purely theological pamphlet; although, as will have been evident, even this is directly connected with the material abuses from which the people were suffering. Another pamphlet of about the same date deals with usury, the burden of which had been greatly increased by the growth of the new commercial combinations already referred to in the Introduction, which combinations Dr. Eck had been defending at Bologna on theological grounds, in order to curry favour with the Augsburg merchant-prince, Fugger-schwatz.[1] It is called "Concerning Dues. Hither comes a poor peasant to a rich citizen. A priest comes also thereby, and then a monk. Full pleasant to read." A peasant visits a burgher when he is counting money, and asks him where he gets it all from. "My dear peasant," says the townsman, "thou askest me who give me this money. I will tell thee. There cometh hither a peasant, and beggeth me to lend him ten or twenty gulden. Thereupon I ask him an he possesseth not a goodly meadow or cornfield. 'Yea! good Sir! ' saith he, 'I have indeed a good meadow and a good corn-field. The twain are worth a hundred gulden'. Then say I to him: 'Good, my friend, wilt thou pledge me thy holding? and an thou givest me one gulden of thy money every year I will lend thee twenty gulden now'. Then is the peasant right glad, and saith he: 'Willingly will I pledge it thee'. ' I will warn thee,' say I, ' that an thou furnishest not the one gulden of money each year, I will take thy holding for my own having.' Therewith is the peasant well content, and writeth him down accordingly. I lend him the money; he payeth me one year, or may be twain, the due; thereafter can he no longer furnish it, and thereupon I take the holding and drive away the peasant therefrom. Thus I get the holding and the money. The same things do I with handicraftsmen. Hath he a good house? He pledgeth that house until I bring it behind me. Therewith gain I much in goods and money, and thus do I pass my days." "I thought," rejoined the peasant, "that 'twere only the Jew who did usury, but I hear that ye also ply that trade." The burgher answers that interest is not usury, to which the peasant replies that interest (*Gült*) is only a "subtle name". The burgher then quotes Scripture, as commanding men to help one another. The peasant readily answers that in doing this they have no right to get advantage from the assistance they proffer. "Thou art a good fellow!" Says the townsman. "If I take no money for the money that I lend, how shall I then increase my hoard?" The peasant then reproaches him that he sees well that his object in life is to wax fat on the substance of others; "But I tell thee, indeed," he says, "that it is a great and heavy sin". Whereupon his opponent waxes wroth, and will have nothing more to do with him, threatening to kick him out in the name of a thousand devils; but the peasant returns to the charge, and expresses his opinion that rich men do not willingly hear the truth. A priest now enters, and to him the townsman explains the dispute. "Dear peasant," says the priest, "wherefore camest thou hither, that thou shouldst make of a due[2] usury? May not a man buy with his money what he will?" But the peasant stands by his previous assertion, demanding how anything can be considered as bought which is only a pledge. "We priests," replies the ecclesiastic, "must perforce lend money for dues, since thereby we get our living;" to which, after sundry ejaculations of surprise, the peasant retorts: "Who gave to you the power? I well hear ye have another God than we poor people. We have our Lord Jesus Christ, who hath forbidden such money-lending for gain." Hence it comes, he does on, that land is no longer free; to attempt to whitewash usury under the name of due or interest, he says, is just the same as if one were to call a child christened Friedrich or Hansel, Fritz or Hans, and then maintain it was no longer the same child. They require no more Jews, he says, since the Christians have taken their business in hand. The townsman is once more about to turn the peasant out of his house, when a monk enters. He then lays the matter before the new-comer, who promises to talk the peasant over with soft words; for, says he, there is nothing accomplished with vainglory. He thereupon takes him aside and explains it to him by the illustration of a merchant whose gain on the wares he sells is not called usury, and argues that therefore other forms of vain in business should not be described by this odious name. But the peasant will have none of this comparison; for the merchant, he says, needs to incur much risk in order to gain and traffic with his wares; while money-lending on security is, on the other hand, without risk or labour, and is a treacherous mode of cheating. Finding that they can make nothing of the obstinate countryman, the others leave him; but he, as a parting shot, exclaims: "Ah, Well-a-day! I would to have talked with thee at first, but it is now ended. Farewell, gracious sir, and my other kind sirs. I, poor little peasant, I go my way. Farewell, farewell, due remains usury for evermore. Yea, yea! due, indeed!"

One more example will suffice to give the reader an idea of the character of these first specimens of pamphlet literature;

and this time it shall be taken from the widely-read anonymous tract entitled "Der Karsthans". [The Man who wields the Hoe, that is, the Peasant.] This production is specially- directed against the monk, Murner, who had at first, as already stated, endeavoured to sit on the fence, admitting certain abuses in the Church, but who before long took sides against Luther and the Reformation, becoming, in fact, after the disputation with Eck, the author of a series of polemical writings against the hero of the Reformation. The most important of these appeared in the autumn of 1520; and the "Karsthans" is the answer to them from the popular side of the movement. On the title-page Murner is depicted as a monk with a cat's head; and in the dialogue there are five *dramatis personae*, Karsthans, Murner, Luther, a Student, and Mercury, the latter interjecting sarcastic remarks in Latin. Turner begins by mewing like a cat. Karsthans, the peasant, and his son, the student, listen, and describe to each other the manners and characters of cats, especially, their slyness and cunning. The son at the bidding of his father is about to pelt the cat with stones, but comes back, saying: " Oh, father what a loathsome beast! It is no true cat, though it looketh to be one. It waxeth even greater and greater. Its hue is grey, and it hath a wondrous head." As the father, Karsthans, is seeking his flail that he may annihilate the beast, his son discovers that it is human, at which the father exclaims: "It is a devil!" They advance towards it, and discover it to be a churchman. "I am a clerk and more than a clerk," cries Murner in anger. "I am cke a man and a monk." Karsthans asks pardon; but Murner threatens him, and, as the monk grows more exasperated, the son exhorts the father to modesty in the presence so exalted a spiritual personage. "Oh, father!" cries the son, " It is indeed a great man. I have read his title. He is a poet, who bath been crowned with the laurel wreath, and is a doctor in both disciplines, and also in the Holy Scriptures. Moreover, he is one of the: free regular clergy, and is called Thomas Murner of Strassburg." Some chaff follows between the father and son as to all the monk's spirituality residing in his garb. This gives rise to a quarrel between Karsthans and Murner, in which the student

81

again exhorts his father to moderation in his language, on the ground that Murner is a good jurist. Karsthans demands how it is compatible to be spiritual in the cloister and cunning in the world, to which Murner replies: *Incompatibilia auctoritate papae unici possunt.* ("Incompatibles can be made to agree by the authority of the Pope.") Karsthans, who calls this a lie, is roundly abused by Murner: "Thou boorish clown, *injustum est ut monachis operandibus servi eorum otio torpeunt*". ("It is unjust that while monks are their servants should slumber in idleness.") "Yea, truly!" answers Karsthans, "ye stink of secrets. During the dispute Luther enters. Ah!" exclaims Murner, "doth that fellow come? There are too many people here. Let me go out by the back." Karsthans wonders at Murner's attitude, as in a general way the Churches were glad to meet each other, and as Luther was everywhere recognised as a good man and a pious Christian. Murner begs Karsthans not to reveal him, as he is pledged to regard Luther as a heretic, and he is determined to prove him one. Karsthans wants to know why he does not dispute personally with Luther like "Dr. Genzhuss," meaning Eck, in Leipzig. "But, father," interposes the son, "Dr. Eck, as some say, hath not won for himself much honour or victory- over Luther." Karsthans is amazed, and replies: "But yet he hath so cried out and fought that scarce an one might speak before him". "He hath also," the student observes, "received 500 ducats from the Pope for his works; and," he adds, "if Dr. Eckius had overcome Luther, as he hath been overcome by him, he (that is, the Pope) would have made of him a camel with broad hoofs," the latter being a current phrase to indicate a cardinal; "and Murner also hopes to pluck some feathers out of the crow, like Eck." Luther knocks again, and Murner tries to get away, but Karsthans holds him hack. After sundry pleasantries between Karsthans and Murner, in the course of which the monk advises the peasant to go to the bookseller, Grüninger, in Strassburg, and buy his two books, the one on "Baptism," and the other entitled "A Christian and Brotherly Warning," Murner takes his leave, and Luther enters. On Karsthans wanting to know what brings him to Germany, he replies: "The simplicity of the German people — to wit, that they are of so small an understanding. What any man feigns and lies to them, that they at once believe, and think no further of the matter. Therefore are they so much deceived, and a laughing stock for other peoples." The student reminds his father that Murner had declared Luther to be a heretic. Karsthans thereupon again seeks his flail; but Luther demands impartiality. Since he had heard Murner he should hear him also. Karsthans agrees; but the son objects, as the Dominicans and doctors in Cologne, especially Hochstraten,[3] had said that it was dangerous to dispute with or, give ear to such people, since even the *Ketzermeister* (refuters of heretics) often came off second best in the contest; as in the case of Dr. Reuchlin, who in spite of their condemnation had been exonerated by Rome, and the Papal sentence against him revoked. "And again what a miracle happened in the 20th year at Mainz! There came a legate from Rome, who was to see that Luther's books were thoroughly burnt; and while all were awaiting the issue at the appointed place, the hangman asked whether judgement had been given that the books should be burnt; and since no one could tell him the truth, the careless fellow would not execute the sentence, and went his way. Oh! what great shame and ignominy was shown to the legate! And since he was not willing to bear the shame, he must persuade the hangman with cunning and presents that he should the next day burn two or four little books. I had thought," concluded the student, "that he had not need to have asked further in the face of the Pope's legate and strict command, and of the heretic-confuter's office." Karsthans is indignant, and threatens every "rascal from home" with his flail; to which the student rejoins: "Oh, father ! thou thinkest it is with the Pope's power as with thy headship in the village which thou hast, where thou canst not of thy will act a straw's breadth except with the knowledge and consent of thy neighbours, who are all vile peasants, and who think there will be sore trouble if they judge other than as witness-bearing dictateth. But it is not so with the Pope; ofttimes it is: *Sic volumus, sic jubemus, oportet; sufficit, vicisse*. ("As we

will, as we command, so let it be; it sufficeth to have prevailed.")
Karsthans requires that if the Pope has divine power, he should
also do divine works; whereas the student defends the absolute
power of the Pope and the bishops. He complains that his father
is an enemy of the priests, like all the rest of the peasants.
Karsthans rejoins that there are four propositions on which the
whole controversy turns: "Thou art Peter; on St. Peter I will build
my Church. Feed my sheep. What I bid you, that do ye. He who
despiseth you, despiseth me also." He then demands of Luther
that he should write in the German tongue, and let them see
whether they could not save him from the power of the Pope and
from the wearers of broad-brimmed hats. But Luther declines
such help, and thereupon departs. Karsthans is offended that the
Pope is called by his son, the student, the highest authority of the
Christian faith. "For," says he, "Christ alone is this authority. He
is the only bridegroom, and the bride can know no other. Else
were she impure and wrinkled, and not a pure bride. Moreover,
the bride is not at variance with her bridegroom, but with the
Pope she is well-nigh always at variance. That which one will,
the other will not. Furthermore, the bride is spiritual, but this
Roman is bodily and worldly." The student answers: "The
bridegroom hath given the bride a bodily head," a point which the
peasant disputes, while admitting it may be good to have spiritual
and carnal authority; "but," says he, "Christ has called to this
office not only one but all the Apostles," and he enlarges on the
difference between this and the scramble for office then apparent
in the State. The student again remonstrates with his peasant
father for his unceremonious treatment of the learned man; and,
at the same time, he blames Luther for attacking certain articles
of the Christian faith, which all 1men ought to hold sacred.
Karsthans wants to know if he refers to the dogma of the Trinity.
This the student denies, saying that it is no such thing as that, or
any other question which the theologians seek to prick with the
point of a needle. He finally admits that he is referring to the
question of the supremacy of the Pope, affirming that it "were a
deadly sin to believe that the Pope had stood one quarter of an

hour in deadly sin. Item, that the Pope alone shall interpret the right sense and meaning of the Scriptures, and shall alone have full power, not only on earth, but also in Purgatory." The student then proceeds to quote the various Credos, the Athanasian, the Nicene, and so forth; till at last Karsthans bursts out: "Look you now! if you make it so, the articles of faith will at last be a great bookful. ... The pious doctor, Martin Luther, doth teach aright: 'Rest thy faith on Christ alone, and therewith hath the matter an end'. "Karsthans, in addition, proceeds to uphold the right of the common man to his own interpretation of the articles of faith, maintaining the appeal to Holy Writ against all ecclesiastical authority; "for by the Scripture one knoweth unfailingly at all time whether such authority do rule righteously or not, since the Scripture is the true article of covenant which Christ hath left us ". The dispute continues, with occasional interjections in Latin by Mercury, in his capacity as cynical chorus, till Karsthans gets very rude indeed, accuses the absent Murner of having lice in his cowl, calls him an evil cat that licks before and scratches behind, and demands why he dare not go to Wittenberg to dispute with Dr. Martin Lather, as Eck had just done. Then with an *Aldi, ich far dakin*, equivalent to the modern English, "Well, I'm off," from the peasant, a *Dii secundent* from Mercury, and an *Uterque* valeat from the student, the party separates, and the dialogue comes to an end.

We have given a somewhat lengthy account of this dialogue, on account of its importance, even at the risk of wearying the reader. Its drastic assertion of the right of the common man to independence of his superiors in spiritual matters, with its side hints and suggestions justifying resistance to all authority that had become oppressive, was not without its effects on the social movements of the following years. For the reader who wishes to further study this literature we give the titles, which sufficiently indicate their contents, of a selection of other similar pamphlets and broadsheets: '' A New Epistle from the Evil Clergy sent to their righteous Lord, with an answer from their Lord. Most merry to read " (152 t). "A Great Prize which the Prince of Hell, hight Lucifer, now offereth to the Clergy, to the Pope, Bishops, Cardinals, and their like" (1521). ''A Written Call, made by the Prince of Hell to his clear devoted, of all and every condition in his kingdom " (1521). "Dialogue or Converse of the Apostolicum, Angelica, and other spices of the Druggist, anent Dr. Martin Luther and his disciples" (1521). "A Very Pleasant Dialogue and Remonstrance from the Sheriff of Gaissdorf and his pupil against the pastor of the same and his assistant" (1521). The popularity of "Karsthans" amongst the people is illustrated by the publication and wide distribution of a new "Karsthans" a few months later, in which it is sought to show that the knighthood should make common cause with the peasants, the *dramatis personae* being Karsthans and Franz von Sickingen. Referring to the same subject we find a "Dialogue which Franciscus von Sickingen held fore heaven's gate with St. Peter and the knights of St. George before he was let in ". This was published in 152;, almost immediately after the death of Sickingen. "A Talk between a Nobleman, a Monk, and a Courtier" (1525). "A Talk between a Fox and a Wolf" (1523). "A Pleasant Dialogue between Dr. Martin Luther and the cunning Messenger from Hell" (1523). "A Conversation of the Pope with his Cardinals of how it goeth with him, and how he may destroy the Word of God. Let every man very well note" (t125). "A Christian and Merry Talk, that it is more pleasing to God and more wholesome for men to come out of the monasteries and to marry, than to tarry therein and to burn; which talk is not with human folly and the false teachings thereof, but is founded alone in the holy, divine, biblical and evangelical Scripture" (1524). "A Pleasant Dialogue of a Peasant with a Monk that he should cast his Cowl from him. Merry and fair to read" (1525).

The above is only a selection of specimens taken haphazard from the mass of fugitive literature which the early years of the Reformation brought forth. In spite of certain rough but not unattractive directness of diction, a prolonged reading of them is very tedious, as will have been sufficiently seen from the extracts we have given. The humour is of a particularly juvenile and obvious character, and consists almost entirely in the childish device of clothing the personages with ridiculous but non-essential attributes, or in placing them in grotesque but pointless situations. Of the more subtle humour, which consists in the discovery of real but hidden incongruities, and the perception of what is innately absurd, there is no trace. The obvious abuses of the time are satirised in this way *ad nauseam*. The rapacity of the clergy in general, the idleness and lasciviousness of the monks, the pomp and luxury of the prince-prelates, the inconsistencies of Church traditions and practices with Scripture, with which they could now be compared, since it was everywhere circulated in the vulgar tongue, form their never-ending theme. They reveal to the reader a state of things that strikes one none the less in English literature of the period, — the intense interest of all classes in theological matters. It shows us how they looked at all things through a theological lens. Although we have left this phase of popular thought so recently behind us, we can even now scarcely imagine ourselves back into it. The idea of ordinary men, or of the vast majority, holding their religion as anything else than a very pious opinion absolutely unconnected with their daily life, public or private, has already become almost inconceivable to us. In all the writings of the time, the theological interest is in the forefront. The economic and social ground-work only casually reveals itself. This it is that makes the reading of the sixteenth century polemics so insufferably jejune and dreary. They bring before us the ghosts of controversies in which most men have ceased to take any part, albeit they have not been dead and forgotten long enough to have acquired a revived antiquarian interest. It reminds one of the faint echoes of the doctrinal disputes of a generation ago, which, already dying on the Continent of Europe, still continued to agitate the English middle classes of all ranks, and are remembered now with but a smile at their immense puerility.

87

The great bomb-shell which Luther cast forth on the 24th of June, 1520, in his address to the German nobility,[4] indeed contains strong appeals to the economical and political necessities of Germany, and therein we see the veil torn from the half-unconscious motives that lay behind the theological mask; but, as already said, in the popular literature, with a few exceptions, the theological controversy rules undisputed.

The noticeable feature of all this irruption of the *cacoëthes scribendi* was the direct appeal to the Bible for the settlement not only of strictly theological controversies but of points of social and political ethics also. This practice, which even to the modern Protestant seems insipid and played out after three centuries and a half of wear, had at that time the to us inconceivable charm of novelty; and the perusal of the literature and controversies of the time shows that men used it with all the delight of a child with a new toy, and seemed never tired of the game of searching out texts to justify their position. The diffusion of the whole Bible in the vernacular, itself a consequence of the rebellion against priestly tradition and the authority of the Fathers, intensified the revolt by making the pastime possible to all ranks of society.

Footnotes

1. See Appendix C.

2. We use the word "due" here for the German word *Gült*. The corresponding, English of the time does not make any distinction between *Gült* or interest, and *Wucher* or usury.

3. Hochstraten was one of the great adversaries of Reuchlin.

4. "An der Christlichen Adel deutscher Nation."

IV. The Folklore of the Reformation

Now in the hands of all men, the Bible was not made the basis of doctrinal opinions alone. It lent its support to many of the popular superstitions of the time, and in addition it served as the starting point for new superstitions and for new developments of the older ones. The Pan-daemonism of the New Testament, with its wonder- workings by devilish agencies, its exorcisms of evil spirits and the like, could not fail to have a deep effect on the popular mind. The authority that the book believed to be divinely inspired necessarily lent to such beliefs have a vividness to the popular conception of the devil and his angels, which is apparent throughout the whole movement of the Reformation, and not least in the utterances of the great Luther himself. Indeed, with the Reformation there curves a complete change over the popular conception of the devil and diabolical influences.

It is true that the judicial pursuit of witches and witchcraft, in the earlier Middle Ages only a sporadic incident, received a great impulse from the Bull of Pope Innocent VIII. (1484), to which has been given the title of "Malleus maleficorum," or "The Hammer of Witchcraft," directed against the practice of sorcery; but it was especially amongst the men of the New Spirit that the belief in the prevalence of compacts with the devil, and the necessity for suppression them, took root, and led to the horrible persecutions that distinguished the "Reformed" Churches on the whole even more than the Catholic.

Luther himself had a vivid belief, tinging all his views and actions, in the ubiquity of the devil and his myrmidons. "The devils," says he, "are near us, and do cunningly contrive every moment without ceasing against our life, our salvation, and our blessedness ..... In woods, waters, and wastes, and in damp, marshy places, there are many devils that seek to harm men. In the black and thick clouds, too, there are some that make storms, hail, lightning, and thunder, that poison the air and the pastures.

When such things happen, the philosophers and the physicians ascribe them to the stars, and show I know not what causes for such misfortunes and plagues." Luther relates numerous instances of personal encounters that he himself had had with the devil. A nobleman invited him, with other learned men from the University of Wittenberg, to take part in a hare hunt. A large, fine hare and a fox crossed the path. The nobleman, mounted on a strong, healthy steed, dashed after them, when, suddenly, his horse fell dead beneath him, and the fox and the hare flew up in the air and vanished. "For," says Luther, "they were devilish spectres."

Again, on another occasion, he was at Eisleben on the occasion of another hare-hunt, when the nobleman succeeded in killing eight hares, which were, on their return home, duly hung up for the next day's meal. On the following morning, horses' heads were found in their place. "In mines," says Luther, "the devil oftentimes deceives men with a false appearance of gold." All disease and all misfortune were the direct work of the devil; God, who was all good, could not produce either. Luther gives a long history of how he was called to a parish priest, who complained of the devil's having created a disturbance in his house by throwing the pots and pans about, and so forth, and of how he advised the priest to exorcise the fiend by invoking his own authority as a pastor of the Church.

At the Wartburg, Luther complained of having been very much troubled by the Satanic arts. When he was at work upon his translation of the Bible, or upon his sermons, or engaged in his devotions, the devil was always making disturbances on the stairs or in the room. One day, after a hard spell of study, he lay down to sleep in his bed, when the devil began pelting him with hazel nuts, a sack of which had been brought to him a few hours before by an attendant. He invoked, however, the name of Christ, and lay down again in bed. There were other more curious and more doubtful recipes for driving away Satan and his emissaries. Luther is never tired of urging that contemptuous treatment and rude chaff are among the most efficacious methods.

There was, he relates, a poor soothsayer, to whom the devil came in visible form, and offered great wealth provided that he would deny Christ and never more do penance. The devil provided him with a crystal, by which he could foretell events, and thus become rich. This he did; but Nemesis awaited him, for the devil deceived him one day, and caused him to denounce certain innocent persons as thieves. In consequence, he was thrown into prison, where he revealed the compact that he had made, and called for a confessor. The two chief forms in which the devil appeared were, according to Luther, those of a snake and a sheep. He further goes into the question of the population of devils in different countries. On the top of the Pilatus at Luzern is a black pond, which is one of the devil's favourite abodes. In Luther's own country there is also a high mountain, the Poltersberg, with a similar pond. When a stone is thrown into this pond, a great tempest arises, which often devastates the whole neighbourhood. He also alleges Prussia to be full of evil spirits.

Devilish changelings, Luther said, were often placed by Satan in the cradles of human children. "Some maids he often plunges into the water, and keeps them with him until they have borne a child." These children are placed in the beds of mortals, and the true children are taken out and hurried away. " But," he adds, "such changelings are said not to live more than to the eighteenth or nineteenth year." As a practical application of this, it may be mentioned that Luther advised the drowning of a certain child of twelve years old, on the ground of its being a devil's changeling. Somnambulism is, with Luther, the result of diabolical agency. "Formerly," says he, "the Papists, being superstitious people, alleged that persons thus afflicted had not been properly baptised, or had been baptised by a drunken priest." The irony of the reference to superstition, considering the "great reformer's" own position, will not be lost upon the reader.

Thus, not only is the devil the cause of pestilence, ,but he is also the immediate agent of nightmare and of nightsweats. At

Mölburg in Thuringen, near Erfurt, a piper, who was accustomed to pipe at weddings, complained to his priest that the devil had threatened to carry him away and destroy him, on the ground of a practical joke played upon some companions, to wit, for having mixed horse-dung with their wine at a drinking bout. The priest consoled him with many passages of Scripture anent the devil and his ways, with the result that the piper expressed himself satisfied as regarded the welfare of his soul, but apprehensive as regarded that of his body, which was, he asserted, hopelessly the prey of the devil. In consequence of this, he insisted on partaking of the Sacrament. But the devil had indicated to him when he was going to be fetched, and watchers were accordingly placed in his room, who sat in their armour and with their weapons, and read the Bible to him. Finally, one Saturday at midnight, a violent storm arose, that blew out the lights in the room, and hurled the luckless victim out of a narrow window into the street. The sound of fighting and of armed men was heard, but the piper had disappeared. The next morning he was found in a neighbouring ditch, with his arms stretched out in the form of a cross, dead and coal-black. Luther vouches for the truth of this story, which he alleges to have been told him by a parish priest of Gotha, who had himself heard it from the parish priest of Mölburg, where the event was said to have taken place.

Amongst the numerous anecdotes of a supernatural character told by "Dr. Martin" is one of a "poltergeist." or "Robin Goodfellow," who was exorcised by two nnonks from the guest-chamber of an inn, and who offered his services to them in the monastery. They gave him a corner in the kitchen. The serving-boy used to torment him by throwing dirty water over him. After unavailing protests, the spirit hung the boy up to a beam, but let him down again before serious harm resulted. Luther states that this "brownie" was well known by sight in the neighbouring town (the name of which he does not give. But by far the larger number of his stories, which, be it observed, are warranted as ordinary occurrences, as to the possibility of which there was no question, are coloured by that more sinister side of supernaturalism so much emphasised by the new theology.

The medieval devil was, for the most part, himself little more than a prankish Rübezahl, or Robin Goodfellow; the new Satan of the Reformers was, in very deed, an arch-fiend, the enemy of the human race, with whom no truce or parley might be held. The old folklore belief in *incubi* and *succubi* as the parents of changelings is brought into connection with the theory of direct diabolic begettal. Thus Luther relates how Friedrich, the Elector of Saxony, told him of a noble family that had sprung from a *succubus*: "Just," says he, " as the Melusina at Luxembourg was also such a *succubus*, or devil ". In the case referred to, the *succubus* assumed the shape of the man's dead wife, and lived with him and bore him children, until, one day, he swore at her, when she vanished, leaving only her clothes behind. After giving it as his opinion that all such beings and their offspring are wiles of the devil, he proceeds: "It is truly a grievous thing that the devil can so plague men that he begetteth children in their likeness. It is even so with the nixes in the water, that lure a man therein, in the shape of wife or maid, with whom he doth dally and begetteth offspring of them." The change whereby the beings of the old naive folklore are transformed into the devil or his agents is significant of that darker side of the new theology, which was destined to issue in those horrors of the witchcraft-mania that reached their height at the beginning of the following century.

One more story of a "changeling" before we leave the subject. Luther gives us the following as having come to his knowledge near Halberstadt, in Saxony. A peasant had a baby, who sucked out its mother and five nurses, besides eating a great deal. Concluding that it was a changeling, the peasant sought the advice of his neighbours, who suggested that he should take it on a pilgrimage to a neighbouring shrine of the Mother of God. While he was crossing a brook on the way, an impish voice from under the water called out to the infant, whom he was carrying in a basket. The brat answered from within the basket, "Ho, ho!" and the peasant was unspeakably shocked. When the voice from the water proceeded to ask the child what it was after, and received the answer from the hitherto inarticulate babe that it was going to be laid on the shrine of the Mother of God, to the end that it might prosper, the peasant could stand it no longer, and flung basket and baby into the brook. The changeling and the little devil played for a few moments with each other, rolling over and over, and crying "Ho, ho, ho!" and then they disappeared together. Luther says that these devilish brats may be generally known by their eating and drinking too much, and especially by their exhausting their mother's milk but they may not develop any certain signs of their true parentage until eighteen or nineteen years old. The Princess of Anhalt had a child which Luther imagined to be a changeling, and he therefore advised its being drowned, alleging that such creatures were only lumps of flesh animated by the devil or his angels. Some one spoke of a monster which infested the Netherlands, and which went about smelling at people like a dog, and whoever it smelt died. But those that were smelt did not see it, albeit the bystanders did. The people had recourse to vigils and masses. Luther improved the occasion to protest against the "superstition" of masses for the dead, and to insist upon his favourite dogma of faith as the true defence against assaults of the devil.

Among the numerous stories of Satanic compacts, we are told of a monk who ate up a load of hay, of a debtor who bit off the leg of his Hebrew creditor and ran off to avoid payment, and of a woman who bewitched her husband so that he vomited lizards. Luther observes, with especial reference to this last case, that lawyers and judges were far too pedantic with their witnesses and with their evidence; that the devil hardens his clients against torture, and that the refusal to confess under torture ought to be of itself sufficient proof of dealings with the prince of darkness. "Towards such," says he, "we should show no mercy; I would burn them myself." Black magic or witchcraft he proceeds to characterise as the greatest sin a human being can be guilty of, as, in fact, high treason against God Himself — *crimen laesae majestatis divinae*.

The conversation closes with a story of how Maximilian's father, the Emperor Friedrich, who seems to have obtained a reputation for magic arts, invited a well-known magician to a banquet, and on his arrival fixed claws on his hands and hoofs on his feet by his cunning. His guest, being ashamed, tried to hide the claws under the table as long as he could, but finally he had to show them, to his great discomfiture. But he determined to have his revenge, and asked his host whether he would permit him to give proofs of his own skill. The Emperor assenting, there at once arose a de noise outside the window. Friedrich sprang up from the table, and leaned out of the casement to see what was the matter. Immediately an enormous pair of stag's horns appeared on his head, so that he could not draw it back. Finding the state of the case, the Emperor exclaimed: "Rid me of them again! Thou hath won!" Luther's comment on this was that he was always glad to see one devil getting the best of another, as it showed that some were stronger than others.

All this belongs, roughly speaking, to the side of the matter which regards popular theology; but there is another side which is connected more especially with the New Learning. This other school, which sought to bring the somewhat elastic elements of the magical theory of the universe into the semblance of a systematic whole, is associated with such names as those of Paracelsus, Cornelius Agrippa, and the Abbot von Trittenheim. The fame of the first named was so great throughout Germany that when he visited any town the occasion was looked upon as an event of exceeding importance.[1] Paracelsus fully shared in the beliefs of his age, in spite of his brilliant insights on certain occasions. What his science was like may be imagined when we learn that he seriously speaks of animals who conceive through the mouth, of basilisks whose glance is deadly, of petrified storks changed into snakes, of the still-born young of the lion which are

95

afterwards brought to life by the roar of their sire, of frogs falling in a shower of rain, of ducks transformed into frogs, and of men born from beasts; the menstruation of women he regarded as a venom whence proceeded flies, spiders, earwigs and all sorts of loathsome vermin; night was caused, not by the absence of the sun, but by the presence of the stars, which were the positive cause of the darkness. He relates having seen a magnet capable of attracting the eyeball from its socket as far as the tip of the nose; he knows of salves to close the mouth so effectually that it has to be broken open again by mechanical means, and he writes learnedly on the infallible sighs of witchcraft. By mixing horse-dung with human semen he believed he was able to produce a medium from which, by chemical treatment in a retort, a diminutive human being or *homunculus*, as he called it, could be produced. The spirits of the elements, the sylphs of the air, the gnomes of the earth, the salamanders of the fire, and the undines of the water, were to him real and undoubted existences in nature.

Strange as all these beliefs seem to us now, they were a very real factor in the intellectual conceptions of the Renaissance period, no less than of the MiddleAges, and amidst them there is to be found at times a foreshadowing of more modern knowledge. Many other persons were also more or less associated with the magical school, amongst them Franz von Sickingen. Reuchlin himself, by his Hebrew studies, and especially by his introduction of the Kabbala to Gentile readers, also contributed a not unimportant influence in determining the course of the movement. The line between the so-called black magic, or operations conducted through the direct agency of evil spirits, and white magic, which sought to subject nature to the human will by the discovery of her mystical and secret laws, or the character of the quasi-personified intelligent principles under whose form nature presented herself to their minds, had never throughout the Middle Ages been very clearly defined. The one always had a tendency to shade off into the other, so that even Roger Bacon's practices were, although not condemned, at least looked upon somewhat doubtfully by the Church. At the time of which we treat, however, the interest in such matters had become universal amongst all intelligent persons. The scientific imagination at the close of the Middle Ages and during the Renaissance period was mainly occupied with three questions: the discovery of the means of transmuting the baser metals into gold, or otherwise of producing that object of universal desire; to discover the Elixir Vitae, by which was generally understood the invention of a drug which would have the effect of curing all diseases, restoring man to perennial youth, and, in short, prolonging human life indefinitely; and, finally, the search for the Philosopher's Stone, the happy possessor of which would not only be able to achieve the first two, but also, since it was supposed to contain the quintessence of all the metals, and therefore of all the planetary influences to which the metals corresponded, would have at his command all the forces which mould the destinies of men. In especial connection with the latter object of research may be noted the universal interest in astrology, whose practitioners were to be found at every Court, from that of the Emperor himself to that of the most insignificant prince or princelet, and whose advice was sought and carefully heeded on all important occasions. Alchemy and astrology were thus the recognised physical sciences of the age, under the auspices of which a Copernicus and a Tycho Brahe were born and educated.

Footnotes

1. Cf. Sebastian Franck, *Chronica,* for an account of a visit of Paracelsus to Nürnberg.

V. The German Town

From what has been said the reader may form for himself an idea of the intellectual and social life of the German town of the period. The wealthy patrician class, whose mainstay politically was the *Rath,* gave the social tone to the whole. In spite of the sharp and sometimes brutal fashion in which class distinctions asserted themselves then, as throughout the Middle ages, there was none of that aloofness between class and class which characterises the bourgeois society of the present day. Each town, were it great or small, was a little world in itself, so that every citizen knew every other citizen more or less. The schools attached to its ecclesiastical institutions were: practically free of access to all the children whose parents could find the means to maintain them during their studies; and consequently the intellectual differences between the different classes were by no means necessarily proportionate to the difference in social position. So far as culture and material prosperity were concerned, the towns of Bavaria and Franconia, Munich, Augsburg, Regensburg, and perhaps above all Nürnberg, represented the high-water mark of medieval civilisation as regards town-life. On entering the burg, should it have happened to be in time of peace and in daylight, the stranger would clear the drawbridge and the portcullis without much challenge, passing along streets lined with the houses and shops of the burghers, in whose open frontages the master and his apprentices and *gesellen* plied their trades, discussing eagerly over their work the politics of the town, and at this period probably the theological questions which were uppermost in men's minds, our visitor would make his way to some hostelry, in whose courtyard he would dismount from his horse, and, entering the common room, or Stube, with its rough but artistic furniture of carved oak, partake of his flagon of wine or beer, according to the district in which he was travelling, whilst the host cracked a rough and possibly coarse jest with the other guests, or narrated to them the latest gossip of the city. The stranger would probably find himself before long the object of interrogatories respecting his native place and the object of his journey (although his dress would doubtless have given general evidence of this, whether he were a merchant or a travelling scholar or a practiser of medicine; for into one of these categories it might be presumed the humble but not servile traveller would fall. Were he on a diplomatic mission from some potentate he would be travelling at the least as a knight or a noble, with spurs and armour, and moreover would be little likely to lodge in a public house of entertainment.

In the *Stube* he would probably see drinking heavily, representatives of the ubiquitous *Landsknechte,* the mercenary troops enrolled for imperial purposes by the Emperor Maximilian towards the end of the previous century, who in the intervals of war were disbanded and wandered about spending their pay, and thus constituted an excessively disintegrative element in the life of the time. A contemporary writer[1] describes them as the curse of Germany, and stigmatises them as "unchristian, God-forsaken folk, whose hand is ever ready in striking, stabbing, robbing, burning, slaying, gaming, who delight in wine-bibbing, whoring, blaspheming, and in the making of widows and orphans ".

Presently perhaps a noise without indicates the arrival of a new guest. All hurry forth into the courtyard, and their curiosity is more keenly whetted when they perceive by the yellow knitted scarf round the neck of the new-comer that he is an *itinerans scholasticus,* or travelling scholar, who brings with him not only the possibility of news from the outer world, so important in an age when journals were non-existent, and communications irregular and deficient, but also a chance of beholding wonder-workings, as well as of being cured of the ailments which local skill had treated in vain. Already surrounded by a crowd of admirers waiting for the words of wisdom to fall from his lips, he would start on that exordium which bore no little resemblance to the patter of the modern quack, albeit interlarded with many a Latin quotation and great display of medieval learning. "Good

100

people and worthy citizens of this town," he might say, "behold in me the great master ... prince of necromancers, astrologer, second mage, chiromancer, agromancer; pyromancer, hydromancer. My learning is so profound that were all the works of Plato and Aristotle lost to the world, I could from memory restore them with more elegance than before. The miracles of Christ were not so great as those which I can perform wherever and as often as I will. Of all alchemists I am the first, and my powers are such that I can obtain all things that man desires. My shoebuckles contain more learning than the heads of Galen and Avicenna, and my beard has more experience than all your high schools. I am monarch of all learning. I can heal you of all diseases. By my secret arts I can procure you wealth. I am the philosopher of philosophers. I can provide you with spells to bind the most potent of the devils in Hell. I can cast your nativities and foretell all that shall befall you, since I have that which can unlock the secrets of all things that have been, that are, and that are to come."[2] Bringing forth strange-looking phials, covered with cabalistic signs, a crystal globe and an astrolabe, followed by an imposing scroll of parchment inscribed with mysterious Hebraic-looking characters, the travelling student would probably drive a roaring trade amongst the assembled townsmen in love-philtres, cures for the ague and the plague, and amulets against them, horoscopes, predictions of fate and the rest of his stock-in-trade.

As evening approaches, our traveller strolls forth into the streets and narrow lanes of the town, lined with overhanging gables that almost meet overhead and shut out the light of the afternoon sun, so that twilight seems already to have fallen. Observing that the burghers, with their wives and children, the work of the day being done, are all wending toward the western gate, he goes along with the stream till, passing underneath the heavy portcullis and through the outer rampart, he finds himself in the plain outside, across which a rugged bridlepath leads to a large quadrangular meadow, rough and more or less worn, where a considerable crowd has already assembled. This is the *Allerwiese*, or public pleasure ground of the town. Here there are not only high festivities on Sundays and holidays, but every fine evening in summer numbers of citizens gather together to watch the apprentices exercising their strength in athletic feats, and competing with one another in various sports, such as running, wrestling, spear-throwing, sword-play, and the like, wherein the inferior rank sought to imitate and even emulate the knighthood, whilst the daughters of the city watched their progress with keen interest and applauding laughter. As the shadows deepen and darkness falls upon the plain, our visitor joins the groups which are now fast leaving the meadow, and reprises the great embrasure just as the rushlights begin to twinkle in the windows, and a swinging oil-lamp to cast a dim light here and there in the streets. But as his company passes out of a narrow lane debouching on to the chief market-place their progress is stopped by the sudden rush of a mingled crowd of unruly apprentices and journeymen returning from their sports, with hot heads well beliquored. Then from another side street there is a sudden flare of torches borne aloft by guildsmen come out to quell the tumult and to send off the apprentices to their dwellings, whilst the watch also bears down and carries off some of the more turbulent of the journeymen to pass the night in one of the towers which guard the city wall. At last, however, the visitor reaches his inn by the aid of a friendly guildsman and his torch; and retiring to his chamber with its strawcovered floor, rough oaken bedstead, hard mattress, and coverings not much better than horse-cloths, he falls asleep as the bell of the minster tolls out ten o'clock over the now dark and silent city.

Such approximately would have been the view of a German city in the sixteenth century as presented to a traveller in a time of peace. More stirring times, however, were as frequent, times when the tocsin rang out from the steeple all night long, calling the citizens to arms. By such scenes, needless to say, the year of the Peasant War was more than usually characterised. In the days when every man carried arms and knew how to use them, when the fighting instinct was imbibed with the mother's milk, when every week saw some street brawl, often attended by loss of life, and that by no means always among the most worthless and dissolute of the inhabitants, every dissatisfaction immediately turned itself into an armed revolt, whether it were of the apprentices or the journeymen against the guild-masters, the body of the townsmen against the patriciate, the town itself against its feudal superior, where it had one, or of the knighthood against the princes. The extremity to which disputes can at present be carried without resulting in a breach of the peace, as evinced in modern political and trade conflicts, exacerbated though some of them are, was a thing unknown in the Middle Ages, and indeed to any considerable extent until comparatively recent times. The sacred right of insurrection was then a recognised fact of life, and but very little straining of a dispute led to a resort to arms. In the subsequent chapters we have to deal with the more important of those outbursts to which the ferment due to the dissolution of the mediaeval system of things, then beginning throughout Central Europe, gave rise, of which the religious side is represented by what is known as the Reformation.

Footnotes

1. Sebastian Franck, *Chronica*, ccxvii.

2. Cf. Trittheim's letter to Wirdung of Hasfurt regarding Faust. *J Trittheimii Epistolarum Familiarum*, 1536, bk.ii., ep.47; also the works of Paracelsus.

VI. The Revolt of the Knighthood

We have already pointed out in more than one place the position to which the smaller nobility, or the knighthood, had been reduced by the concatenation of causes which was bringing about the dissolution of the old medieval order of things, and, as a consequence, ruining the knights both economically and politically: — economically by the rise of capitalism as represented by the commercial syndicates of the cities; by the unprecedented power and wealth of the city confederations, especially of the Hanseatic League; by the rising importance of the newly-developed world-market; by the growing luxury and the enormous rise in the prices of commodities concurrently with the reduction in value of the feudal land-tenures; and by the limitation of the possibilities of acquiring wealth by highway robbery, owing to imperial constitutions on the one hand and increased powers of defence on the part of the trading community on the other politically, by the new modes of warfare in which artillery and infantry, composed of comparatively well-drilled mercenaries *(Landsknechte),* were rapidly making inroads into the omnipotence of the ancient feudal chivalry, and reducing the importance of individual skill or prowess in the handling of weapons, and by the development of the lower of the princes or higher nobility, partly due to the influence which the Roman civil law now began to exercise over the older customary constitution of the Empire, and partly to the budding centralism of authority — which in France and England became a national centralisation, but in Germany, in spite of the temporary ascendancy of Charles V., finally issued in a provincial centralisation in which the princes were *de facto* independent monarchs. The imperial constitution of 1495, forbidding private war, applied, it must be remembered, only to the lesser nobility and not to the higher, thereby placing the former in a decidedly ignominious position as regards their feudal superiors. And though this particular enactment had little immediate result, yet it was none the less resented as a blow struck at the old knightly privilege.

The mental attitude of the knighthood in the face of this progressing change in their position was naturally an ambiguous one, composed partly of a desire to hark back to the haughty independence of feudalism, and partly of sympathy with the growing discontent among other classes and with the new spirit generally. In order that the knights might succeed in recovering their old or even in maintaining their actual position against the higher nobility, the princes, backed as these now largely were by the imperial power, the co-operation of the cities was absolutely essential to them, but the obstacles in the way of such a co-operation proved insurmountable. The towns hated the knights for their lawless practices, which rendered trade unsafe and not infrequently cost the lives of the citizens. The knights for the most part, with true feudal hauteur, scorned and despised the artisans and traders who had no territorial family name and were unexercised in the higher chivalric arts. The grievances of the two parties were, moreover, not identical, although they had their origin in the same causes. The cities were in the main solely concerned to maintain their old independent position, and especially to curb the growing disposition at this time of the other estates to use them as milch cows from which to draw the taxation necessary to the maintenance of the Empire. For example, at the Reichstag opened at Nürnberg on the 17th November, 1522 to discuss the questions of the establishment of perpetual peace within the Empire, of organising an energetic resistance to the inroads of the Turks, and of placing on a firm foundation the Imperial Privy Council (*Kammergericht*) and the Supreme Council (*ReichsRegiment*) — at which were represented twenty-six imperial towns, thirty-eight high prelates, eighteen princes, and twenty-nine counts and barons — the representatives of the cities complained grievously that their attendance was reduced to a farce, since they were always out-voted, and hence obliged to accept the decisions of the other estates. They stated that their position was no longer bearable; and for the first time drew up, an Act of Protest, which further complained of the delay in the decisions of the imperial courts; of their sufferings from the right of private war which was still allowed to subsist in defiance of the constitution; of the increase of customs-stations on the part of the princes and prince-prelates; and, finally, of the debasement of the coinage due to the unscrupulous practices of these notables and of the Jews. The only sympathy the other estates vouchsafed to the plaints of the cities was with regard to the right of private war, which the higher nobles were also anxious to suppress amongst the lower, though without prejudice of course to their own privileges in this line. All the other articles of the Act of Protest were coolly waived aside. From all this it will be seen that not much co-operation was to be expected between such heterogeneous bodies as the knighthood and the free towns, in spite of their common interest in checking the threateningly advancing power of the princes and the central imperial authority, which was for the most part manned and manipulated by the princes.

Amid the decaying knighthood there was, as we have already intimated, one figure which stood out head and shoulders above every other noble of the time, whether prince or knight; and that was Franz von Sickingen. He has been termed, not without truth, "the last flower of German chivalry," since in him the old knightly qualities flashed up in conjunction with the old knightly power and splendour with a brightness hardly known even in the palmiest days of medieval life. It was, however, the last flicker of the light of German chivalry. With the death of Sickingen and the collapse of his revolt the knighthood of Central Europe ceased any longer to play an independent part in history.

Sickingen, although technically only one of the lower nobility, was deemed about the time of Luther's appearance to hold the immediate destinies of the Empire in his hand. Wealth, inspiring confidence and enthusiasm as a leader, possessed of more than one powerful and strategically-situated stronghold, he held court at his favourite residence, the Castle of the Landstuhl, in the Rhenish Palatinate, in a style which many a prince of the Empire might have envied. As honoured guests were to be found attending on him, humanists, poets, minstrels, partisans of the new theology, astrologers, alchemists, and men of letters generally; in short, the whole intelligence and culture of the period. Foremost among these, and chief confidant of Sickingen, was the knight, courtier, poet, essayist and pamphleteer, Ulrich von Hutten, whose pen was ever ready to champion with unstinted enthusiasm the cause of the progressive ideas of his age. He first took up the cudgels against the obscurantists on behalf of Humanism as represented by Erasmus and Reuchlin, the latter of whom he bravely defended in his dispute with the Inquisition and the monks of Cologne, and in his contributions to the *Epistolae Obscurorum Virorum* we see the youthful ardour of the Renaissance in full blast in its onslaught on the forces of medieval obstruction. Unlike most of those with whom he was first associated, Hutten passed from being the upholder of the New Learning to the role of champion of the Reformation; and it was largely through his influence that Sickingen took up the cause of Luther and his movement.

Sickingen had been induced by Charles V. to assist him in an abortive attempt to invade France in 1521, from which campaign he had returned without much benefit either material or moral, save that Charles was left heavily in his debt. The accumulated hatred of generations for the priesthood had made Sickingen a willing instrument in the hands of the reforming party and believing that Charles now lay to some extent in his power, he considered the moment opportune for putting his long-cherished scheme into operation for reforming the constitution of the Empire. This reformation consisted, as was to be expected, in placing his own order on a firm footing, and of effectually curbing the power of the other estates, especially that of the prelates. Sickingen wished to make the Emperor and the lower nobility the decisive factors in his new scheme of things political. The Emperor, it so happened, was for the moment away in Spain, and Sickingen's colleagues of the knightly order were becoming clamorous at the unworthy position into which they found themselves rapidly being driven. The feudal exactions of their princely lieges had reached a point which passed all endurance, and since they were practically powerless in the Reichstags no outlet was left for their discontent save by open revolt. Impelled not less by his own inclinations than by the pressure of his companions, foremost among whom was Hutten, Sickingen decided at once to open the campaign.

Hutten, it would appear, attempted to enter into negotiations for the co-operation of the towns and of the peasants. So far as can be seen, Strassburg and one or two other imperial cities returned favourable answers; but the precise measure of Hutten's success cannot be ascertained, owing to the fact that all the documents relating to the matter perished in the destruction of Sickingen's Castle of Ebernburg. It is certain, however, that operations were begun before any definite assurances of help had been obtained, although had the first attempts had any appearance of success there is little doubt that such help would have been forthcoming.

The campaign was unfortunate from the beginning. Nevertheless, but one of the associated knights saw that the moment was inopportune. The rest were confident of success, and a pretext was speedily found in the fact that Sickingen's feudal superior, the Archbishop of Trier (Treves), had refused to compel two councillors of that city to repay him 5,000 Rhenish guilders (*gülden*) which he had paid as ransom for them to a certain knight, Gerhard Börner, who had taken them prisoners. This was a sufficient *casus belli* for those times; and Sickingen thereupon issued a manifesto in which he declared himself the champion of the gospel, and announced his intention to free the subjects of the archbishop from the temporal yoke of their tyrant, who had acted against God and the imperial majesty, and from the spiritual yoke of godless priests, and to place them in possession of that liberty which the gospel (*i.e.*, the new gospel of Luther alone could afford.

It should be premised that on the 13th of August, previous to this declaration of war, a "Brotherly Convention" had been signed by a number of the knights, by which Sickingen was appointed their captain, and they bound themselves to submit to no jurisdiction save their own, and pledged themselves to mutual aid in war in case of hostilities against any one of their number. Through this "Treaty of Landau," Sickingen had it in his power to assemble a considerable force at a moment's notice. Consequently, a few days after the issue of the above manifesto, on the 27th August, 1522, Sickingen was able to start from the Castle of Ebernburg with an army of 5000 foot and 1,500 knights, besides artillery, in the full confidence that he was about to destroy the position of the Palatine prince-prelate and raise himself without delay to the chief power on the Rhine. The grand chamberlain of the celebrated patron of letters and Humanism, Albrecht, Archbishop of Mainz, Frowers von Hutten, was in the conspiracy; and it is almost certain that Albrecht himself was secretly in accord with Sickingen's plan for the destruction of his electoral neighbour. This is shown by the fact that when the Archbishop of Trier appealed to him, as his colleague, for assistance, Albrecht made a number of excuses which enabled him to delay the sending of reinforcements until they were too late to be of any use, whilst at the same time numbers of his retainers and subjects served under Sickingen's banner.

By an effective piece of audacity, that of sporting the imperial flag and the Burgundian cross, Franz spread abroad the idea that he was acting on behalf of the Emperor, then absent in Spain; and this largely contributed to the result that his army speedily rose to 5,000 knights and 10,000 footmen. The Imperial Diet at Nürnberg now intervened, and ordered Sickingen to cease the operations he had already begun, threatening him with the ban of the Empire and a fine of 2000 marks if he did not obey. To this summons Franz sent a characteristically impudent reply,[1] and light-heartedly continued the campaign, regardless of the warning which an astrologer had given him some time previously, that the year 1522 or 1523 would probably be fatal to him. It is evident that this campaign, begun so late in the year, was regarded by Sickingen and the other leaders as merely a preliminary canter to a larger and more widespread movement the following spring, since on this occasion the Swabian and Franconian knighthood do not appear to have been even invited to take part in it.

After an easy progress, during which several trifling places, the most important being St. Wendel, were taken, Franz with his army arrived on the 8th of September before the gates of Trier. He had hoped to capture the town by surprise, and was indeed not without some expectation of co-operation and help from the citizens themselves. On his arrival he shot letters within the walls summoning the inhabitants to take his part against their tyrant; but either through the unwillingness of the burghers to act with the knights, or through the vigilance of the archbishop, they were without effect. The gates remained closed; and in answer to Sickingen's summons to surrender, Richard replied that he would find him in the city if he could get inside. In the meantime Sickingen's friends had signally failed in their attempts to obtain supplies and reinforcements for him, in the main owing to the energetic action of some of the higher nobles. The Archbishop of Trier showed himself as much a soldier as a churchman; and after a week's siege, during which Sickingen made five assaults on the city, his powder ran out, and he was forced to retire. He at once made his way back to Ebernburg, where he intended to pass the winter, since he saw that it was useless to continue the campaign, with his own army diminishing and the hoped-for supplies not appearing, whilst the forces of his antagonists augmented daily. In his stronghold of Ebernburg he could rely on being secure from all attack until he was able to again take the field on the offensive, as he anticipated doing in the spring.

There is some doubt as to the events which occurred during this retreat to Ebernburg. Sickingen's adversaries asserted that not only did his army destroy churches and monasteries, but

111

that the houses of the peasants in the surrounding country were plundered and burnt. His friends, on the other hand, maintain with equal vehemence that Sickingen and his followers confined themselves to wiping out of existence as many as possible of the hated ecclesiastical foundations.

In spite of the obvious failure of the autumnal campaign, the cause of the knighthood did not by any means look irretrievably desperate, since there was always the possibility of successful recruitments the following spring. Ulrich von Hutten was doing his utmost in Würtemberg and Switzerland to scrape together men and money, though up to this time without much 'success, while other emissaries of Sickingen were working with the same object in Breisgau and other parts of Southern Germany. Relying on these expected reinforcements, Franz was confident of victory when he should again take the field, and in the meantime he felt himself quite secure in one or other of his strong places, which had recently undergone extensive repairs and seemed to be impregnable. In this anticipation he was deceived, as will shortly be seen, for he had not reckoned with the new and more potent weapons of attack which were replacing the battering-ram and other medieval besieging appliances.

The princes, meanwhile, were not inactive. Immediately after the abortive attack on Richard of Trier, Sickingen was placed under the ban of the Empire (Oct. 8), but although the latter had temporarily disbanded his army it was impossible for them to attack him at once. They therefore contented themselves for the moment by wreaking their vengeance on those of his supporters who were more easily to be reached. Albrecht of Mainz, whose public policy had been that of "sitting on the fence all round," was fined 25,000 gulden for his lukewarmness supporting his colleague, the Elector of Trier. Kronberg, near Frankfort, which was held by Sickingen's son-in-law, Hardtmuth, was taken by a force of 40,000 men (?); Frowen von Hutten, the cousin of Ulrich, was driven from his Castle of Saalmünster and dispossessed of his estates, whilst a number of the smaller fry equally felt the heavy hand of the princely power. The chastisement of more distant adherents to the cause of the knighthood, like the Counts of Fürstenberg and Zollern and the knights of Franconia, was left over until the leader of the movement had been dealt with.

This latter task was set about energetically, as soon as the winter was past, by the three princes who had specially taken in hand the suppression of the revolt, Archbishop Richard of Trier, Prince Ludwig of the Pfalz, and Count Phillip of Hesse. In February, Sickingen's second son, Hans, was taken prisoner, and shortly after the Castle of Wartenberg was captured. An armistice which Sickingen had asked for in order that the reinforcements he expected might have time to arrive, was refused, since the princes saw that their only chance of immediately crushing his power was to attack him at once. Towards the end of April a large army of cavalry, infantry, and siege artillery was called together at Kreuznach, not far from Sickingen's Castle of Ebernburg. Franz, however, was no longer there. He appears to have left Ebernburg for his strongest fortress at Landstuhl some weeks previously, though how and when is uncertain. Here he hoped to be able to hold out for at least three or four months, by which time his friends could deliver him; and when the army of the three princes appeared before the castle he sent back a mocking answer to their summons to surrender, to the effect that he had new walls and they had new guns, so they could now see which were the stronger. But Sickingen had not realised the power of the new projectiles; and in a week after the opening of the bombardment, on the 29th of April, the newly-fortified castle on which he had staked all his hopes was little better than a defenceless heap of ruins. In the course of the bombardment Franz himself, as he stood at an embrasure watching the progress of the siege, was flung against a splintered joist, owing to the gun-stand against which he was leaning being overturned by a cannon shot. With his side torn open he was carried down into a dark rocky vault of the castle, realising at last that all was lost. "Where are now," he cried, "my knights and my friends, who promised me so much and who have performed so little? Where is Fürstenberg? where Zollern? where are they of Strassburg and of the Brotherhood? Wherefore, let none place their trust in great possessions nor in the encouragements of men." It must be alleged, however, in their excuse, that his friends doubtless shared Franz's confidence in the impregnability of the Landstuhl, and were not aware of the imminent straits he had been in since the beginning of the attack. The messenger he had sent to the distant Fürstenberg had been captured by the army of the allied princes; Zollern knew of the need of his leader only with the news of his death; Hutten's efforts to obtain help in Switzerland had been in vain.

Seeing that now all was over and he himself on the point of death, Sickingen wrote to the princes, requesting them to come and see him. The firing at once ceased, and negotiations were entered upon for the surrender of the castle. On the 6th of May Sickingen agreed to the articles of capitulation, which included the surrender of himself and the rest of the knights in the castle as prisoners of war, his other retainers giving up their arms and leaving the castle on the following day. The Landstuhl with all its contents was to fall, of course, into the hands of the besiegers. As Franz signed the articles, he remarked to the ambassadors: "Well, I shall not he long your prisoner."

On the 7th of May the princes entered the castle and were at once taken to the underground chamber where Franz lay dying. He was so near his end that he could scarcely distinguish his three arch-enemies one from the other. "My dear lord," he said to the Count Palatine, his feudal superior, "I had not thought that I should end thus," taking off his cap and giving him his hand. "What has impelled thee, Franz," asked the Archbishop of Trier, "that thou halt so laid waste and harmed me and my poor people?" "Of that it were too long to speak," answered Sickingen, "but I have done nought without cause. I go now to stand before a greater Lord." Here it is worthy of remark that the princes treated Franz with all the knightliness and courtesy which were customary between social equals in the days of chivalry, addressing him at most rather as a rebellious child than as an insurgent subject. The prince of Hesse was about to give utterance to a reproach, but he was interrupted by the Count Palatine, who told him that he must not quarrel with a dying man. The count's chamberlain said some sympathetic words to Franz, who replied to him: "My dear chamberlain, it matters little about me. It is not I who am the cock round which they are dancing." When the princes had withdrawn, his chaplain asked him if he would confess; but Franz replied: "I have confessed to God in my heart," whereupon the chaplain gave him absolution; and as he went to fetch the host "the last of the knights" passed quietly away, alone and abandoned. It is related by Spalatin that after his death some peasants and domestics placed his body in an old armour-chest, in which they had to double the head on to the knees. The chest was then let down by a rope from the rocky eminence on which stood the now ruined castle, and was buried beneath small chapel in the village below.

The scene we have just described in the castle vault meant not merely the tragedy of a hero's death, nor merely the destruction of a faction or puny. It meant the end of an epoch. With Sickingen's death one of the most salient and picturesque elements in the mediaeval life of Central Europe received its death-blow. The knighthood as a distinct factor in the polity of Europe henceforth existed no more.

Spalatin relates that on the death of Sickingen the princely party anticipated as easy a victory over the religious revolt as they had achieved over the knighthood. "The mock Emperor is dead," so the phrase went, "and the mock pope will soon be dead also." Hutten, already an exile in Switzerland, did not many months survive his patron and leader, Sickingen. The role which Erasmus played in this miserable tragedy was only what was to be expected from the moral cowardice which seemed ingrained in the character of the great Humanist leader. Erasmus had already begun to fight shy of the Reformation movement, from which he was about to separate himself definitely. He seized the present opportunity to quarrel with Hutten; and to Hutten's somewhat bitter attacks on him in consequence he replied with ferocity in his *Spongia Erasmi adversus aspergines Hutteni*.

Hutten had had to fly from Basel to Mülhausen and thence to Zürich, in the last stages of syphilitic disease. He was kindly received by the reformer, Zwingli of Zürich, who advised him to try the waters of Pfeffers, and gave him letters of recommendation to the abbot of that place. He returned, in no wise benefited, to Zürich, when Zwingli again befriended the sick knight, and sent him to a friend of his, the "reformed" pastor of the little island of "Ufenau," at the other end of the lake, where after a few weeks' suffering he died in abject destitution, leaving, it is said, nothing behind him but his pen. The disease from which Hutten suffered the greater part of his life, at that time a comparatively new importation and much more formidable even than nowadays, may well have contributed to an irascibility of temper and to a certain recklessness which the typical free-lance of the Reformation in its early period exhibited. Hutten was never a theologian, and the Reformation seems to have attracted him mainly from its political side as implying the assertion of the dawning feeling of German nationality as against the hated enemies of freedom of thought and the new light, the clerical satellites of the Roman see. He was a true son of his time, in his vices no less than in his virtues; anti no one will deny his partiality for "wine, women, and play ". There is reason, indeed, to believe that the latter at times during his later career provided his sole means of subsistence.

The hero of the Reformation, Luther, with whom Melancthon may be associated in this matter, could be no less pusillanimous on occasion than the hero of the New Learning, Erasmus. Luther undoubtedly saw in Sickingen's revolt a means of weakening the Catholic powers against which he had to fight, and at its inception he avowedly favoured the enterprise. In "Karsthans," the brochure quoted from in the last chapter, Luther is represented as the incarnation of Christian resignation and mildness, and as talking of twelve legions of angels and deprecating any appeal to force as unbefitting the character of an evangelical apostle. That such, however, was not his habitual attitude is evident to all who are in the least degree acquainted with his real conduct and utterances. On one occasion he wrote: "If they (the priests) continue their mad ravings it seems to me that there would be no better method and medicine to stay them than that kings and princes did so with force, armed themselves and attacked these pernicious people who do poison all the world, and once for all did make an end of their doings with weapons not with words. For even as we punish thieves with the sword, murderers with the rope, and heretics with fire, wherefore do we not lay hands on these pernicious teachers of damnation, on popes, on cardinals, bishops, and the swarm of the Roman Sodom — *yea, with every weapon which lieth within our reach, and wherefore do we not wash our hands in their blood?*"

It is, however, in a manifesto published in July, 1522, just before Sickingen's attack on the Archbishop of Trier, for which enterprise it was doubtless intended as a justification, that Luther expresses himself in unmeasured terms against the "biggest wolves," the bishops, and calls upon "all dear children of God and all true Christians "to drive them out by force from the sheep-stalls". In this pamphlet. entitled "Against the falsely called spiritual order of the Pope and the bishops." he says: "It were better that every bishop were murdered, every foundation or cloister rooted out, than that one soul should be destroyed, let alone that all souls should be lost for the sake of their worthless trumpery and idolatry. Of what use are they who thus live in lust, nourished by the sweat and labour of others, and are a stumbling block to the word of God? They fear bodily uproar and despise spiritual destruction. Are they wise and honest people ? If they accepted God's word and sought the life of the soul, God would be with them, for He is a God of peace, and they need fear no uprising; but if they will not hear God's word, but rage and rave

117

with bannings, burnings, killings, and every evil, what do they better deserve than a strong uprising which shall sweep them from the earth? And we would smile did it happen. As the heavenly wisdom with: "Ye have hated my chastisement and despised my doctrine; behold, I will also laugh at ye in your distress, and will mock ye when misfortune shall fall upon your heads'." In the same document he denounces the bishops as an accursed race, as "thieves, robbers, and usurers". Swine, horses, stones, and wood were not so destitute of understanding as the German people under the sway of them and their Pope. The religious houses are similarly described as "brothels, low taverns, and murder dens". He winds up this document, which he calls his bull, by proclaiming that "all who contribute body, goods, and honour that the rule of the bishops may be destroyed are God's dear children and true Christians, obeying God's command and fighting against the devil's order;" and on the other hand, that "all who give the bishops a willing obedience are the devil's own servants, and fight against God's order and law".[2]

No sooner, however, did things begin to look bad with Sickingen than Luther promptly sought to disengage himself from all complicity or even sympathy with him and his losing cause. So early as the 19th of December, 1522, he writes to his friend Wenzel Link: "Franz von Sickingen has begun war against the Palatine. It will be a very bad business." (*Franciscus Sickingen Palatino bellum indixit, res pessima futura est.*) His colleague, Melancthon, a few days later, hastened to deprecate the insinuation that Luther had had any part or lot in initiating the revolt. "Franz von Sickingen," he wrote, "by his great ill-will injures the cause of Luther; and notwithstanding that he be entirely dissevered from him, nevertheless whenever he undertaketh war he wisheth to seem to act for the public benefit, and not for his own. He is even now pursuing, a most infamous course of plunder on the Rhine." In another letter he says: "I know how this tumult grieveth him (Luther),"[3] and this respecting the man who had shortly before written of the princes, that their

118

tyranny and haughtiness were no longer to be borne, alleging that God would not longer endure it, and that the common man even was becoming intelligent enough to deal with them by force if they did not mend their manners. A more telling example of the "don't-put-him-in-the-horse-pond" attitude could scarcely be desired. That it was characteristic of the "great reformer" will be seen later on when we find him pursuing a similar policy anent the revolt of the peasants.

After the fall of the Landstuhl all Sickingen's castles and most of those of his immediate allies and friends were of course taken, and the greater part of them destroyed. The knighthood was now to all intents and purposes politically helpless and economically at the door of bankruptcy, owing to the suddenly changed conditions of which we have spoken in the Introduction and elsewhere as supervening since the beginning of the century: the unparalleled rise in prices, concurrently with the growing extravagance, the decline of agriculture in many places, and the increasing burdens put upon the knights by their feudal superiors, and last, but not least, the increasing obstacles in the way of the successful pursuit of the profession of highway robbery. The majority of them, therefore, clung with relentless severity to the feudal dues of the peasants, which now constituted their main, and in many cases their only, source of revenue; and hence, abandoning the hope of independence, they threw in their lot with the authorities, the princes, lay and ecclesiastic, in the common object of both, that of reducing the insurgent peasants to complete subjection.

Some few of the more chivalrous knights, foremost among whom was Florian Geyer, retained their rebel instincts against the higher authorities, and took sides with the popular movement. They fought, however, in a forlorn hope. As we shall now see, provincial centralism, as in Italy, and not national centralism as in France, England, and Spain, was destined to be the political form dominant in Germany far into the modern period. The disasters and discomfitures of the Peasants' War,

119

which we shall presently describe, removed the last obstacle to the complete ascendancy of the provincial potentates, the princes of the Empire; for this event was the immediate cause of the final disintegration of medieval life, and the undermining of the last survivals of the free institutions of the communal village which had lasted throughout the Middle Ages.

Footnotes

1. Franz said to the bystanders when the messengers of the Council appeared: "ook at these old fiddles of the *Regiment*; only the dancers lack. There is no dearth of commands, but only of those who heed them;" and turning to the nuncios themselves, he bade them tell the Imperial Stadthalter and the other gentlemen of the Council that "they might make themselves easy, for he was as good a servant of the Emperor as themselves. He would, if he had enough followers, so work it that the Emperor would be able to get far more land and gold in Germany than he could ever get abroad. He only meant to give Richard of Trier a slight drubbing, and to soak his crowns for him which he had gotten from France."

2. *Sämmatliche Werke*, vol. xxviii., 142-201.

3. Corpus Reformatorum, i., 598-599

VII. Country and Town at the End of the Middle Ages

For the complete understanding of the events which follow it must be borne in mind that we are witnessing the end of a distinct historical period; and, as we have pointed out in the Introduction, the expiring effort, half conscious and half unconscious, of the people to revert to the conditions of an earlier age. Nor can the significance be properly gauged unless a clear conception is obtained of the differences between country and town life at the beginning of the sixteenth century. From the earliest periods of the Middle Ages of which we have any historical record, the *Markgenossenschaft*, or primitive village community of the Germanic race, was overlaid by a territorial domination, imposed upon it either directly by conquest or voluntarily accepted for the sake of the protection indispensable in that rude period. The conflict of these two elements, the mark organisation and the territorial lordship, constitutes the marrow of the social history of the Middle Ages.

In the earliest times the pressure of the overlord, whoever he might be, seems to have been comparatively slight, but its inevitable tendency was for the territorial power to extend itself at the expense of the rural community. It was thus that in the tenth and eleventh centuries the feudal oppression had become thoroughly settled, and had reached its greatest intensity all over Europe. It continued thus with little intermission until the thirteenth century, when from various causes, economic and otherwise, matters began to improve in the interests of the common man, till in the fifteenth century the condition of the peasant was better than it has ever been, either before or since within historical times, in Northern and Western Europe. But with all this, the oppressive power of the lord of the soil was by no means dead. It was merely dormant, and was destined to spring into renewed activity the moment the lord's necessities supplied a sufficient incentive. From this time forward the element of territorial power, supported in its claims by the Roman law, with its basis of private property, continued to eat into it until it had finally devoured the old rights and possessions of the village community. The executive power always tended to be transferred from its legitimate holder, the village in its corporate capacity, to the lord; and this was alone sufficient to place the villager at his mercy.

At the time of the Reformation, owing to the new conditions which had arisen and had brought about in a few decades the hitherto unparalleled rise in prices, combined with the unprecedented ostentation and extravagance more than once referred to in these pages, the lord was supplied with the requisite incentive to the exercise of the power which his feudal system gave him. Consequently, the position of the peasant rapidly changed for the worse; and although at the outbreak of the movement not absolutely *in extremis*, according to our notions, yet it was so bad comparatively to his previous condition and that less than half a century before, and tended so evidently to become more intolerable, that discontent became everywhere rife, and only awaited the torch of the new doctrines to set it ablaze. The whole course of the movement shows a peasantry not downtrodden and starved, but proud and robust, driven to take up arms not so much by misery and despair as by the deliberate will to maintain the advantages which were rapidly slipping away from them.

Serfdom was not by any means universal. Many free peasant villages were to be found scattered amongst the manors of the territorial lords, though it was but too evidently the settled policy of the latter at this time to sweep everything into their net, and to compel such peasant communes to accept a feudal over-lordship. Nor were they at all scrupulous in the means adopted for attaining their ends. The ecclesiastical foundations, as before said, were especially expert in forging documents for the purpose of proving that these free villages were lapsed feudatories of their own. Old rights of pasture were being curtailed, and others, notably those of hunting and fishing, had in most manors been completely filched away.

It is noticeable, however, that although the immediate causes of the peasant rising were the new burdens which had been laid upon the common people during the last few years, once the spirit of discontent was aroused it extended also in many cases to the traditional feudal dues to which until then the peasant had submitted with little murmuring, and an attempt was made by the country side to reconquer the ancient complete freedom of which a dim remembrance had been handed down to them.

The condition of the peasant up to the beginning of the sixteenth century, that is to say, up to the time when it began to so rapidly change for the worse, may be gathered from what we are told by contemporary, writers, such as Wimpfeling, Sebastian Brandt, Wittenweiler, the satires in the *Nürnberger Fastnachspielen*, and numberless other sources; as also from the sumptuary laws of the end of the fifteenth century. All these indicate an ease and profuseness of living which little accord with our notions of the word peasant. Wimpfeling writes: "The peasants in our district and in many parts of Germany have become, through their riches, stiff-necked and ease-loving. I know peasants who at the weddings of their sons or daughters, or the baptism of their children, make so much display that a house and field might be bought therewith, and a small vineyard to boot. Through their riches, they are oftentimes spendthrift in food and in vestments, and they drink wines of price."

A chronicler relates of the Austrian peasants, under the date of 1478, that "they wore better garments and drank better wine than their lords"; and a sumptuary law passed at the Reichstag, held at Lindau in 1497, provides that the common peasant man and the labourer in the towns or in the field "shall neither make nor wear cloth that costs more than half a gulden the ell, neither shall they wear gold, pearls, velvet, silk, nor embroidered clothes, nor shall they permit their wives or their children to wear such".

Respecting the food of the peasant, it is stated that he ate his full in flesh of every kind, in fish, in bread, in fruit, drinking wine often to excess. The Swabian, Heinrich Müller, writes in the year 1550, nearly two generations after the change had begun to take place: "In the memory of my father, who was a peasant man, the peasant did eat much better than now. Meat and food in plenty was there every day, and at fairs and other junketings the tables did well-nigh break with what they bore. Then drank they wine as it were water, then did a man fill his belly and carry away withal as much as he could; then was wealth and plenty. Otherwise is it now. A costly and a bad time hath arisen since many a year, and the food and drink of the best peasant is much worse than of yore that of the day labourer and the serving man."

We may well imagine the vivid recollections which a peasant in the year 1525 had of the golden days of a few years before. The day labourers and serving men were equally tantalised by the remembrance of high wages and cheap living at the beginning of the century. A day labourer could then earn, with his keep, nine, and without keep, sixteen groschen[1] a week. What this would buy may he judged from the following prices current in Saxony during the second half of the fifteenth century. A pair of good working shoes cost three groschen; a whole sheep, four groschen; a good fat hen, half a groschen; twenty-five cod fish, four groschen; a waggon-load of firewood, together with carriage, five groschen; an ell of the best homespun cloth, five groschen; a scheffel (about a bushel of rye, six or seven groschen. The Duke of Saxony wore grey hats which cost him four groschen. In Northern Rhineland about the same time a day labourer could, in addition to his keep, earn in a week a quarter of rye, ten pounds of pork, six large cans of milk, and two bundles of firewood, and in the course of five weeks be able to buy six ells of linen, a pair of shoes, and a bag for his tools. In Augsburg the daily wages of an ordinary labourer represented the value of six pounds of the best meat, or one pound of meat, seven eggs, a peck of peas, about a quart of wine, in addition to such bread as he required, with enough over for lodging, clothing, and minor expenses. In Bavaria he could earn daily eighteen pfennige, or one and a half groschen, whilst a pound of sausage cost one pfennig, and a pound of the best beef two pfennige, and similarly throughout the whole of the States of Central Europe.

A document of the year 1483, from Ehrbach in the Swabian Odenwald, describes for us the treatment of servants by their masters. "All journeymen," it declares, "that are hired, and likewise bondsmen (serfs, also the serving men and maids, shall each day be given twice meat and what thereto longith, with half a small measure of wine, save on fast days, when they shall have fish or other food that nourisheth. Whoso in the week bath toiled shall also on Sundays and feast days make merry after mass and preaching. They shall have bread and meat enough, and half a great measure of wine. On feast days also roasted meat enough. Moreover, they shall be given, to take home with them, a great loaf of bread and so much of flesh as two at one meal may eat."

Again, in a bill of fare of the household of Count Joachim von Oettingen in Bavaria, the journeymen and villeins are accorded in the morning, soup and vegetables; at mid-day, soup and meat, with vegetables, and a bowl of broth or a plate of salted or pickled meat; at night, soup and meat, carrots, and preserved meat. Even the women who brought fowls or eggs from the neighbouring villages to the castle were given for their trouble — if from the immediate vicinity, a plate of soup with two pieces of bread; if from a greater distance, a complete meal and a cruise of wine. In Saxony, similarly, the agricultural journeymen received two meals a day, of four courses each, besides frequently cheese and bread at other times should they require it. Not to have eaten meat for a week was the sign of the direst famine in any district. Warnings are not wanting against the evils accruing to the common man from his excessive indulgence in eating and drinking.

Such was the condition of the proletariat in its first

inception, that is, when the mediaeval system of villeinage had begun to loosen and to allow a proportion of free labourers to insinuate themselves into its working. How grievous, then, were the complaints when, while wages had risen either not at all or at most from half a groschen to a groschen, the price of rye rose from six or seven groschen a bushel to about five-and-twenty groschen, that of a sheep from four to eighteen groschen, and all other articles of necessary consumption in a like proportion![2]

In the Middle Ages, necessaries and such ordinary comforts as were to be had at all were dirt cheap; while non-necessaries and luxuries, that is, such articles as had to be imported from afar, were for the most part at prohibitive prices. With the opening up of the world-market during the first half of the sixteenth century, this state of things rapidly changed. Most luxuries in a short time fell heavily in price, while necessaries rose in a still greater proportion.

This latter change in the economic conditions of the world exercised its most powerful effect, however, on the character of the mediaeval town, which had remained substantially unchanged since its first great expansion at the end of the thirteenth and the beginning of the fourteenth centuries. With the extension of commerce and the opening up of communications, there began that evolution of the town whose ultimate outcome was to entirely change the central idea on which the urban organisation was based.

The first requisite for a town, according to modern notions, is facility of communication with the rest of the world by means of railways, telegraphs, postal system, and the like. So far has this gone now that in a new country, for instance America, the railway, telegraph lines, etc., are made first, and the towns are then strung upon them, like beads upon a cord. In the mediaeval town, on the contrary, communication was quite a secondary matter, and more of a luxury than a necessity. Each town was really a self-sufficing entity, both materially and intellectually. The modern idea of a town is that of a mere local aggregate of individuals, each pursuing a trade or calling with a view to the world-market at large. Their own locality or town is no more to them economically than any other part of the world-market, and very little more in any other respect. The medieval idea of a town, on the contrary, was that of an organisation of groups into one organic whole. Just as the village community was a somewhat extended family organisation, so was, *mutatis mutandis*, the larger unit, the township or city. Each member of the town organisation owed allegiance and distinct duties primarily to his guild, or immediate social group, and through this to the larger social group which constituted the civic society. Consequently, every townsman felt a kind of *esprit de corps* with his fellow-citizens, akin to that, say, which is alleged of the soldiers of the old French "foreign legion," who, being brothers-in-arms, were brothers also in all other relations. But if every citizen owed duty and allegiance to the town in its corporate capacity, the town no less owed protection and assistance, in every department of life, to its individual members.

As in ancient Rome in its earlier history, and as in all other early urban communities, agriculture necessarily played a considerable part in the life of most mediaeval towns. Like the villages they possessed each its own mark, with its common fields, pastures, and woods. These were demarcated by various landmarks, crosses, holy images, etc.; and "the bounds" were beaten every year. The wealthier citizens usually possessed gardens and orchards within the town walls, while each inhabitant had his share in the communal holding without. The use of this latter was regulated by the Rath or Council. In fact, the town life of the Middle Ages was not by any means so sharply differentiated from rural life as is implied in our modern idea of a town. Even in the larger commercial towns, such as Frankfurt, Nürnberg or Augsburg, it was common to keep cows, pigs, and sheep, and, as a matter of course, fowls and geese, in large numbers within the precincts of the town itself. In Frankfurt in 1481 the pigsties in the town had become such a nuisance that the

Rath had to forbid them in the front of the houses by a formal decree. In Ulm there was a regulation of the bakers' guild to the effect that no single member should keep more than twenty-four pigs, and that cows should be confined to their stalls at night. In Nürnberg in 1475 again, the Rath had to interfere with the intolerable nuisance of pigs and other farmyard stock running about loose in the streets. Even in a town like München we are informed that agriculture formed one of the staple occupations of the inhabitants, while in almost every city the gardeners' or the winegrowers' guild appears as one of the largest and most influential.

It is evident that such conditions of life would be impossible with town-populations even approaching only distantly those of to-day; and, in fact, when we come to inquire into the size and populousness of mediaeval cities, as into those of the classical world of antiquity, we are at first sight staggered by the smallness of their proportions. The largest and most populous free imperial cities in the fifteenth and sixteenth centuries, Nürnberg and Strassburg, numbered little more than 20,000 resident inhabitants within the walls, a population rather less than that of (say) Gloucester at the present time. Such an important place as Frankfurt-am-Main is stated at the middle of the fifteenth century to have had less than 9,000 inhabitants. At the end of the fifteenth century Dresden could only boast of about 5,000. Rothenburg on the Tauber is to-day a dead city to all intents and purposes, affording us a magnificent example of what a mediaeval town was like, as the bulk of its architecture, including the circuit of its walls, which remain intact, dates approximately from the sixteenth century. At present a single line of railway branching off from the main line with about two trains a day is amply sufficient to convey the few antiquarians and artists who are now its sole visitors, and who have to content themselves with country-inn accommodation. Yet this old free city has actually a larger population at the present day than it had at the time of which we are writing, when it was at the height of its prosperity as an important centre of activity. The figures of its population are now between 8,000 and 9,000. At the beginning of the sixteenth century they were between 6,000 and 7,000. A work written and circulated in manuscript during the first decade of the sixteenth century, "A Christian Exhortation" (*Ein Christliche Mahnung*), after referring to the frightful pestilences recently raging as a punishment from God, observes, in the spirit of true Malthusianism, and as a justification of the ways of Providence, that "an there were not so many that died there were too much folk in the land, and it were not good that such should be lest there were not food enough for all".

Great population as constituting importance in a city is comparatively a modern notion. In other ages towns became famous on account of their superior civic organisation, their more advantageous situation, or the greater activity, intellectual, political, or commercial, of their citizens.

What this civic organisation of mediaeval towns was, demands a few words of explanation, since the conflict between the two main elements in their composition plays an important part in the events which follow. Something has already been said on this head in the Introduction. We have there pointed out that the Rath or Town Council, that is the supreme governing bode of the municipality, was in all cases mainly, and often entirely, composed of the heads of the town aristocracy, the patrician class or "honorability" (*Ehrbarkeit*), as they were termed, who on the ground of their antiquity and wealth laid claim to every post of power and privilege. On the other hand were the body of the citizens enrolled in the various guilds, seeking, as their position and wealth improved, to wrest the control of the town's resources from the patricians. It must be remembered that the towns stood in the position of feudal over-lords to the peasants who held land on the city territory, which often extended for many square miles outside the walls. A small town like Rothenburg, for instance, which we have described above, had on its lands as many as 15,000 peasants. The feudal dues and contributions of these tenants constituted the staple revenue of the town, and the management of them was one of the chief bones of contention.

Nowhere was the guild system brought to a greater perfection than in the free imperial towns of Germany. Indeed, it was carried further in them, in one respect, than in any other part of Europe, for the guilds of journeymen (*Gesellenverbande*), which in other places never attained any strength or importance, were in Germany developed to the fullest extent, and of course supported the craft-guilds in their conflict with the patriciate. Although there were naturally numerous frictions between the two classes of guilds respecting wages, working days, hours, and the like, it must not be supposed that there was that irreconcilable hostility between them which would exist at the present time between a trades union and a syndicate of employers. Each recognised the right to existence of the other. In one case, that of the strike of bakers towards the close of the fifteenth century, at Colmar in Elsass, the craft-guilds supported the journeymen in their protest against a certain action of the patrician Rath which they considered to be a derogation from their dignity.

Like the masters the journeymen had their own guild-house, and their own solemn functions and social gatherings. There were, indeed, two kinds of journeymen-guilds: one whose chief purpose was a religious one, and the other concerning itself in the first instance with the secular concerns of the body. However, both classes of journeymen-guilds worked into one another's hand. On coming into a strange town a travelling member of such a guild was certain of a friendly reception, of maintenance until he procured work, and of assistance in finding it as soon as possible.

Interesting details concerning the wages paid to journeymen and their contributions to the guilds are to be found in the original documents relating exclusively to the journeymen-guilds, collected by Georg Schanz.[3] From these and other sources it is clear that the position of the artisan in the towns was in proportion much better than even that of the peasant at that time, and therefore immeasurably superior to anything he has enjoyed since. In South Germany at this period the average price of beef was about two denarii[4] a pound, while the daily wages of the masons and carpenters, in addition to their keep and lodging, amounted in the summer to about twenty, and in the winter to about sixteen of these denarii. In Saxony the same journeymen-craftsmen earned on the average, besides their maintenance, two groschen four pfennige a day, or about one-third the value of a bushel of corn. In addition to this, in some cases the workman had weekly gratuities under the name of "bathing money"; and in this connection it may be noticed that a holiday for the purpose of bathing once a fortnight, once a week, or even oftener, as the case might be, was stipulated for by the guilds, and generally recognised as a legitimate demand. The common notion of the uniform uncleanliness of the medieval man requires to be considerably modified when one closely investigates the condition of town life, and finds everywhere facilities for bathing in winter and summer alike. Untidiness and uncleanliness, according to our notions, there may have been in the streets and in the dwellings in many cases, owing to inadequate provisions for the disposal of refuse and the like; but we must not therefore extend this idea to the person, and imagine that the mediaeval craftsman or even peasant was as unwholesome as, say, the Roumanian peasant of to-day.

When these wages received by the journeymen artisans are compared with the prices of commodities previously given, it will be seen how relatively easy were their circumstances; and the extent of their well-being may be further judged from the wealth of their guilds, which, although, varying in different places, at all times formed a considerable proportion of the wealth of the town. The guild system was based upon the notion that the individual master and workman was working as much in the interest of the guild as for his own advantage. Each member of the guild was alike under the obligation to labour, and to labour in accordance with the rules laid down by his guild, and at the same time had the right of equal enjoyment with his fellow-guildsmen of all advantages pertaining to the particular branch of industry covered by the guild. Every guildsman had to work himself *in propria persona*, no contractor was tolerated who himself "in ease and sloth doth live on the sweat of others, and puffeth himself up in lustful pride". Were a guild-master ill and unable to manage the affairs of his workshop, it was the council of the guild, and not himself or his relatives, who installed a representative for him and generally looked after his affairs. It was the guild again which procured the raw material, and distributed it in relatively equal proportions amongst its members; or where this was not the case, the time and place were indicated at which the guildsman might buy at a fixed maximum price. Every master had equal right to the use of the common property and institutions of the guild, which in some industries included the essentials of production, as, for example, in the case of the woollen manufacturers, where wool kitchens, carding rooms, bleaching houses and the like were common to the whole guild.

Needless to say, the relations between master and apprentices and master and journeymen were rigidly fixed clown to the minutest detail. The system was thoroughly patriarchal in its character. In the hey-day of the guilds, every apprentice and most of the journeymen regarded their actual condition as a period of preparation which would end in the glories of mastership. For this dear hope they were ready on occasion to undergo cheerfully the most arduous duties. The education in handicraft, and, we may add, the supervision of the morals of the blossoming members of the guild, was a department which greatly exercised its administration. On the other hand, the guild in its corporate capacity was bound to maintain sick or incapacitated apprentices and journeymen, though after the journeymen had developed into a distinct class, and the consequent rise of the journeymen-guilds, the latter function was probably in most cases taken over by them. The guild laws against adulteration, stamped work, and the like, were sometimes ferocious in their severity. For example, in some towns the baker who misconducted himself in the matter of the composition of his bread was condemned to be shut up in a basket which was fixed at the end of along pole, and let down so many times to the bottom of a pool of dirty water. In the year 1456 two grocers, together with a female assistant:, were burnt alive at Nürnberg for adulterating saffron and spices, and a similar instance happened at Augsburg in 1492. From what we have said it will be seen that. guild life, like the life of the town as a whole, was essentially a social life. It was a larger family, into which various blood families were merged. The interest of each was felt to be the interest of all, and the interest of all no less the interest of each.

But in many towns, outside the town population properly speaking, outside the patrician families who generally governed the Rath, outside the guilds, outside the town organisation altogether, there were other bodies dwelling within the walls and forming *imperia in imperiis*. These were the religious corporations, whose possessions were often extensive, and who, dwelling within their own walls, shut out from the rest of the town, were subject only to their own ordinances. The quasi-religious, quasi-military Order of the Teutonic Knights (*Deutscher Orden*), founded at the time of the Crusades, was the wealthiest and largest of these corporations. In addition to the extensive territories which it held in various parts of the Empire, it had establishments in a large number of cities. Besides this there were, of course, the Orders of the Augustinians and Carthusians, and a number of less important foundations, who had their cloisters in various towns. At the beginning of the sixteenth century, the pomp, bride, and licentiousness of the Teutonic Order drew upon it the especial hatred of the townsfolk; and amid the general wreck of religious houses none were more ferociously despoiled than those belonging to this Order. There were, moreover, in some towns, the establishments of princely families, which were regarded by the citizens with little less hostility than that accorded to the religious Orders.

Such were the explosive elements of town life when changing conditions were tending to dislocate the whole structure of mediaeval existence. The capture of Constantinople by the Turks in 1453 had struck a heavy blow at the commerce of the Bavarian cities which had come by way of Constantinople and Venice. This latter city lost one by one its trading centres in the East, and all Oriental traffic by way of the Black Sea was practically stopped. It was the Dutch cities who inherited the wealth and influence of the German towns when Vasco da Gama's discovery of the Cape route to the East began to have its influence on the trade of the world. This diversion of Oriental traffic from the old overland route was the starting point of the modern merchant navy, and it must be placed amongst the most potent causes of the break-up of mediaeval civilisation. The above change, although immediately felt by the German towns, was not realised by them in its full importance either as to its causes or its consequences for more than a century; but the decline of their prosperity was nevertheless sensible, even now, and contributed directly to the coming upheaval.

Footnotes

1. One silver groschen = 11/2d.

2. The authorities for the above data are to be found in Janssen, i., vol. i., bk. iii., especially pp.330-346.

3. *Zur Geschichte der deutsrhen Gesellenverbande*, Leipz., 1876.

4. C. (d. The denarius was the South German equivalent of the North German *pfennig*, of which twelve went to the groschen.

VII. The New Jurisprudence

The impatience of the prince, the prelate, the noble, and they wealthy burgher at the restraints which the system of the Middle Ales placed upon his activity as an individual in the acquisition for his own behoof and the disposal at his own pleasure of wealth, regardless of the consequences to his neighbour, found expression, and a powerful lever, in the introduction from Italy of the Roman law in place of the old canon and customary law of Europe. The latter never regarded the individual as an independent and autonomous entity, but invariably treated him with reference to a group or social body, of which he might be the head or merely a subordinate member; but in any case the filaments of custom and religious duty attached him to a certain humanity outside himself, whether it were a village community, a guild, a township, a province, or the Empire. The idea of a right to individual autonomy in his dealings with men never entered into the medieval man's conception. Hence the mere possession of property was not recognised by mediaeval law as conferring an absolute rights in its holder to its unregulated use, and the basis of the mediaeval notions of property was the association of responsibility and duty with ownership. In other words, the notion of *trust* was never completely divorced from that of *possession*.

The Roman law rested on a totally different basis. It represented the legal ethics of a society on most of its sides brutally and crassly individualistic. That that society had come to an end instead of evolving to its natural conclusion — a developed capitalistic individualism such as exists to-day — was due to the weakness of its economic basis, owing to the limitation at that time of man's power over nature, which deprived it of recuperative and defensive power, thereby leaving it a prey not only to internal influences of decay but also to violent destructive forces from without. Nevertheless, it left a legacy of a ready-

135

made legal system to serve as an implement for the first occasion when economic conditions should be once more ready for progress to resume the course of individualistic development, abruptly brought to an end by the fall of ancient civilisation as crystallised in the Roman Empire.

The popular courts of the village, of the mark and of the town, which had existed up to the beginning of the sixteenth century with all their ancient functions, were extremely democratic in character. Cases were decided on their merits, in accordance with local custom, by a body of jurymen chosen from among the freemen of the district, to whom the presiding functionaries, most of whom were also of popular selection, were little more than assessors. The technicalities of a cut-and-dried system were unknown. The Catholic Germanic theory of the Middle Ages proper, as regards the civil power in all its functions, from the highest downward, was that of the mere administrator of justice as such; whereas the Roman law regarded the magistrate as the vicegerent of the *princeps* or *imperator*, in whose person was absolutely vested as its supreme embodiment the whole power of the State. The Divinity of the Emperors was a recognition of this fact; and the influence of the Roman law revived the theory as far as possible under the changed conditions, in the form of the doctrine of the Divine Right of Kings — a doctrine which was totally alien to the Catholic feudal conception of the Middle Ages. This doctrine, moreover, received added force from the Oriental conception of the position of the ruler found in the Old Testament, from which Protestantism drew so much of its inspiration.

But apart from this aspect of the question, the new juridical conception involved that of a system of rules as the crystallised embodiment of the abstract "State," given through its representatives which could under no circumstances be departed from, and which could only be modified in their operation by legal quibbles that left to them their nominal integrity. The new law could therefore only be administered by a class of men

136

trained specially for the purpose, of which the plastic customary law borne down the stream of history from primitive times, and insensibly adapting itself to new conditions but understood in its broader aspects by all those who might be called to administer it, had little need. The Roman law, the study of which was started at Bologna in the twelfth century, as might naturally be expected, early attracted the attention of the German Emperors as a suitable instrument fur use on emergencies. But it made little real headway in Germany itself as against the early institutions until the fifteenth century, when the provincial power of the princes of the Empire was beginning to overshadow the central authority of the titular chief of the Holy Roman Empire. The former, while strenuously resisting the results of its application from above, found in it a powerful auxiliary in their courts in riveting their power over the estates subject to them. As opposed to the delicately adjusted hierarchical notions of Feudalism, which did not recognise any absoluteness of dominion either over persons or things, in short for which neither the head of the State had any inviolate authority as such, nor private property any inviolable rights or sanctity as such, the new jurisprudence made corner-stones of both these conceptions.

Even the canon law, consisting in a mass of Papal decretals dating from the early Middle Ages, and which, while undoubtedly containing considerable traces of the influence of Roman law, was nevertheless largely customary in its character with an infusion of Christian ethics, had to yield to the new jurisprudence, and that too in countries where the Reformation had been unable to replace the old ecclesiastical dogma and organisation. The principles and practice of the Roman law were sedulously inculcated by the tribe of civilian lawyers who by the beginning of the sixteenth century infested every Court throughout Europe. Every potentate, great and small, little as he might like its application by his feudal over-lord to himself, was yet only too ready and willing to invoke its aid for the oppression of his own vassals or peasants. Thus the civil law everywhere triumphed. It became the juridical expression of the political, economical, and religious change which marks the close of the Middle Ages and the beginnings of the modern commercial world.

It must not be supposed, however, that no resistance was made to it. Everywhere in contemporary literature, side by side with denunciations of the new mercenary troops, the *Landsknechte*, we find uncomplimentary allusions to the race of advocates, notaries, and procurators who, as one writer has it, "are increasing like grasshoppers its town and in country year by year". Wherever they appeared, we are told, countless litigious disputes sprang up. He who had but the money in hand might readily defraud his poorer neighbour in the name of law and right. "Woe is me!" exclaims one author, "in my home there is but one procurator, and yet is the whole country round about brought into confusion by his wiles. What a misery will this horde bring upon us!" Everywhere was complaint and in many places resistance.

As early as 1460 we find the Bavarian estates vigorously complaining that all the courts were in the hands of doctors. They demanded that the rights of the land and the ancient custom should not be cast aside; but that the courts as of old should be served by reasonable and honest judges, who should be men of the same feudal livery and of the same country as those whom they tried. Again in 1514, when the evil had become still more crying, we find the estates of Würtemberg petitioning Duke Ulrich that the Supreme Court "shall be composed of honourable, worthy, and understanding men of the nobles and of the towns, who shall not be doctors, to the intent that the ancient usages and customs should abide, and that it should be judged according to them in such wise that the poor man might no longer be brought to confusion". In many covenants of the end of the fifteenth century, express stipulation is made that they should not be interpreted by a doctor or licentiate, and also in some cases that no such doctor or licentiate should be permitted to reside or to exercise his profession within certain districts. Great as was the economical influence of the new jurists in the tribunals, their political influence in the various courts of the Empire, from the *Reichskammergericht* downwards, was, if anything, greater. Says Wimpfeling , the first writer on the art of education in the modern world: "According to the loathsome doctrines of the new jurisconsults, the prince shall be everything in the land and the people naught. The people shall only obey, pay tax, and do service. Moreover, they shall not alone obey the prince but also those he has placed in authority, who begin to puff themselves up as the proper lords of the land, and to order matters so that the princes themselves do as little as may be reign." From this passage it will be seen that the modern bureaucratic state, in which government is as nearly as possible reduced to mechanism and the personal relation abolished, was ushered in under the auspices of the civil law. How easy it was for the civilian to effect the abolition of feudal institutions may be readily imagined by those cognisant of the principles of Roman law. For example, the Roman law of course making no mention of the right of the mediaeval "estates" to be consulted in the levying of taxes or in other questions, the jurist would explain this right to his too willing master, the prince, as an abuse which had no legal justification, and which, the sooner it were abolished in the interest of good government the better it would be. All feudal rights as against the power of an over-lord were explained away by the civil jurist, either as pernicious abuses, or, at best, as favours granted in the past by the predecessors of the reigning monarch, which it was within his right to truncate or to abrogate at his will.

From the preceding survey will be clearly perceived the important rôle which the new jurisprudence played on the continent of Europe in the gestation of the new phase which history was entering upon in the sixteenth century. Even the short sketch given will be sufficient to show that it was not in one department only that it operated; but that, in addition to its own domain of law proper, its influence was felt in modifying economical, political, and indirectly even ethical and religious conditions. From this time forth Feudalism slowly but surely gave place to the newer order, all that remained being certain of its features, which, crystallised into bureaucratic forms, were doubly veneered with a last trace of medieval ideas and a denser coating of civilian conceptions. This transitional Europe, and not mediaeval Europe, was the Europe which lasted on until the eighteenth century, and which practically came to an end with the French Revolution.

Appendix A

The following is a rescript issued by a Commission of the Reichstag held at Nürnberg in 1522-23, anent the commercial syndicates which the sudden development of the world-market had recently called into existence:-

"What the small Commission by order of the great Commission hath determined concerning the Monopolia or pernicious and prohibited commerce is hereafter related."

(MSS. of 61 pages in the Ernestine General Archives at Weimar, Margin E. Quoted by Egelhaaf. Appendix, vol. i.)

"In the first place, concerning the origin of the word Monopolia. Monopolia is a Greek word, from the word Monos, that is, alone, and Polonia, that is, a selling. As if one should say: I alone sell this or that, or my Company or I alone sell. Therefore, such separate dealing whereby several dealers or traders unite together in such wise that they alone obtain profit from their handicraft or merchandy is called Monopolia. This is discoursed of in Lege Unica (?), Cod. de Monopoliis.

"Item, the aforesaid Monopolia, Uniting, Combining, Associatings and their Sellings have not now for the first time been found not to be borne; but the same were regarded and known as very noxious to the Commonweal, destructive and worthy to be punished, as aforetime by the Roman Emperors and Jurisconsults, and more especially by the blessed Emperor Justinian, so that such trespassers should be made to lose all their goods, and moreover should be adjudged to eternal misery (exile) from their own homes, as standeth written Lege Unica, Cod. de Monop. Honorius also and Theodosius forbade those of noble birth and those of the richer sort from harmful commerce; so that the common folk might the more easily buy of the Merchants; and in the Reichstag at Köln in 1512 the matter was much debated by the Emperor Maximilian, the Electors, the Princes and the Estates, and the aforesaid increase in the price of Wares was forbidden under great pains and penalties. The decree of the Reichstag sayeth:-

"And since much great fellowship in Trade hath arisen within the Realm in the last years, and also there,be several and sundry persons who venture to bring all kinds of Wares and:Merchants' goods, such as Spices, Arras, Woollen Cloth, and such-like into their own hand with power to trade in them, to set or to make their own advantage out of them, as it them pleaseth, and do greatly harm thereby the Holy Empire and all Estates thereof, contrary to the Imperial written Law and to all honesty: we have ordered and enacted for the furthering of the common profit and according to necessity, and we do desire that earnestly, and we will, that such noxious dealing be henceforth forbidden, and that they abstain [from it], and that henceforth they may [not] carry it on or exercise it. Those who shall do this contrary to the aforesaid, their Goods and Chattels shall be confiscated and fall to the Authority of the place. And the same Companies and Merchants [shall] henceforth not be conducted [on their journeys] by any authority in the Empire, nor shall it be lawful for such to do so with whatsoever words, opinion or clauses the convoy hath been given. Yet shall it not be forbidden to any man on this account to enter into company with any other save only if he undertake to bring the Wares into one hand and to place upon the Wares a worth according to his own mind and pleasure; or shall pledge the buyer or seller to sell, to give, or to keep such Wares to or for no man but himself, or that he shall not give them save such wise as he bath agreed with him. But when they, to whom it is permitted to pursue such trade, shall seek to make an unbecoming dearness, the Authority shall with zeal and earnestness forbid such dearness, and command an honest sale; but where an Authority be careless, the Fiscal shall exhort the same to perform his duty within the space of one month, failing such hath the Fiscal power to enter process against him.

"But the Authority and the Fiscal have neither done their duty, as is not right nor just, forasmuch as in the present times other small robbers and thieves are punished sorely, and these rich Companies, even one of them, do in the year compass much more undoing to the Commonweal than all other robbers and thieves in that they and their servants give public display of luxuriousness, pomp and prodigal wealth, of which there is no small proof in that Bartholomew Rhein did win, in so short a time and with so little stock of trade, such notable riches in the Hochstetter Company — as hath openly appeared in the justifying before the City Court at Augsburg and at the Reichstag but lately held at Worms. Therefore hath the said Rhem been made prisoner in Worms, and is even still kept in durance. Moreover shall he be sent here to Nürnberg that he may bear witness, and that it may be known with what perils the aforesaid forbidden Monopolies and Trade be practised, also through what good ways and means such may be set aside and prevented.

"There are three questions to be discoursed of: (1) Whether the Monopolies be hurtful to the Holy Empire and therefore are to be destroyed; (2) Whether all Companies without difference shall be done away, or

143

whether a measure shall be set to them; (3) By what means this shall be done, and how these things may be remedied.

"I. Firstly, that the great Companies and the heaping up of their Stocks are everywhere harmful is the one cause as may be seen from the Spice, which is the most considerable Merchandise thus dealt and traded with, in the German nation. It is said with credibility that the King of Portugal hath not to pay more for one pound's weight of Pepper sent from the Indies to Antwerp than three shillings in gold, twenty of which shillings go to a Rhenish Gulden. But also if a Company in Portugal doth send for Spices it hath no trouble and excuse. How dear soever the King doth offer or give the Wares, it payeth him sometimes yet more, but on condition that he shall not furnish such Wares to them who will hereafter buy, save for a still greater price. To this example it may be added that he who hath offered an hundred-weight of Pepper from Portugal for eighteen ducats hath received for them twenty ducats or even more, with the condition that the Royal Majesty shall furnish to none other for the space of one or two years the same Pepper or Ware, cheaper than twenty-four ducats, and thereby one hath so outbidden the other that the Spice which at the first could be sold but for eighteen ducats is now sold in Portugal for thirty-four ducats and upwards. And it hath become at one time well-nigh as dear as it was ever before. The same hath also happened to other Spices with which such Merchants are nothing burdened, nor do they have any loss therewithal, but great over-abounding gain, the while they, for their part, will sell as dearly as they may, and none else in the Holy Empire may have or obtain the same. What loss and disadvantage resulteth to most men, even to the least, is not hard to be comprehended. We may prove this from the Nürnberg Spice convoys. The Saffron

144

of most price, so called from the Catalonian place Saffra, hath cost some years ago, as namely in the sixteenth year, two and a half Gulden, six Kreutzers; now in the twenty-second year it costeth five and a half Gulden, fifteen Kreutzers. The best Saffron, which is called Zymer by the Merchants, hath cost from 1516 to 1519 two Gulden the pound, and even in 1521 two Gulden, twenty-four to twenty-six Kreutzers; now it costeth four Gulden; and even so are all Saffrons more dear, Arragonian, Polish, Avernian, etcetera.

"The Merchants, moreover, do not make dear everything at the same time, but now with Saffron and Cloves, the one year with Pepper and Ginger, then with Nutmeg, etcetera, to the intent that their advantage may not at once be seen of men. It is therefore purposed to make an enquiry of how much Spices are brought into Germany each year, so that it may be known how much the tax upon these Spices would bring in, in so far as the Merchants make a small increase to each pound, as happeneth very commonly. It hath been ordered to the Merchants to make estimation thereof, but their estimations were diverse; yet are the numbers told for the Spices which each year go in from Lisabon [Lisbon] alone, so that there may be had better knowledge. 36,000 hundred-weight of Pepper and not less but rather the more; 2,400 hundred-weight of Ginger, about 1,000 balls of Saffron do come from Lisabon alone, without that which cometh from Venice. For the other Spices they do not make known the sum. At Antwerp this may be known the more surely, through the due which is there levied.

"The Companies have paid especial note to such Wares as can be the least spared; and if one be not rich enough, it goeth for help to another, and the twain together do bring the Wares, whatsoever they be, wholly into their own hand. If a poor, small Merchant buy of them these same

145

Wares, whose worth hath been cunningly enhanced, and if he desireth to trade with these Wares, according to his needs, then these aforesaid great hucksters are from that hour upon his neck, they have the abundance of these same Wares, and can give them cheaper and on longer borrowing; thereby is this poor man oppressed, cometh to harm and some to destruction. Ofttimes do they buy back their Wares through unknown persons, but not to the gain of them that sell; therefore it is that they have their Storehouses in wellnigh all places in Europe; and here lieth the cause of the magnificence of the heaping up of Stock.

"The great Companies do lessen trading and consuming in the lands. They do all their business in far countries and by letters; where now there is a great Company, there aforetime did twenty or more [persons], it may be, nourish themselves, who must all now wander afar, because they cannot hold a storehouse and servants in other places. By these means came it to pass that roads, tolls and convoy dues were multiplied, as innkeepers and all handiworkers of use and pleasure have knowledge; for many sellers bring good sale and cheapness into the Wares.

"Furthermore, the good gold and silver Monies are brought out of the land by the Companies, who everywhere do buy them up and change them. Within a short time Rhenish gold will have been changed and melted from far-seeking lust of gain. Therefore are there already in divers towns risings of the poor man, which, where it be not prevented, will, it is to be feared, extend further and more.

"II. *Now it be asked, are all Companies to be therefore destroyed?* We have now already shown cause why the great Companies mighty in money should be scattered and not be borne with. I3ut, therefore, it is not said that all

Companies and common trading should be wholly cut away; this were indeed against the Commonweal and very burdensome, harmful and foolish to the whole German nation; for therefrom would follow (1) that one should give strength, help and fellowship to Frenchmen and foreign nations, that they should undertake and carry out that which with so much pains we have gone forth to destroy. These foreign nations would then suck out the whole German land. (2) Furthermore, if each would trade singly and should lose thereby, that would then be to his undoing, and also to theirs who had entrusted to him their Goods. That may not happen where divers persons join together with moderation. (3) Such a forbidding would solely serve the rich to their advantage, who in all cases everywhere do pluck the grain for themselves and do leave the chaff for others. Of these rich, some are so placed that they are able even to do that which now great Companies do and which is thought to be so sore an oppression. Therewith would the matter not be bettered, but only a covering would be set upon it. (4) Trading and industry do bring this with them, that the Wares should not be sought in one place alone. One man is not able, and more especially not at the time when there is need thereof. The issue would be that trade in the land would be forbidden and it would serve the gain of foreign nations, and especially at this time [hurt?] the Germans; but to hire servants and to send such in his stead to another place needs money, and small Stocks will hardly bear the holding of domestics; many there be, indeed, who are not able to provide for themselves, let alone for servants.

"III. What proposals are now to be put forth for the staying of the aforesaid forbidden practice?

"(1) Companies or single persons shall use no more than twenty thousand, forty thousand, or for the most fifty thousand Gulden Stock for trade, and shall have no more

147

than three Storehouses outside their family dwelling.

"(2) They shall be held by their bodily sworn vows to declare to their Authority that they have no more money in trade.

"(3) Their Stock may not be enhanced by gain; but rather, at farthest, account must be made every two years and the gain divided, also a notifying to the Authority must be made that the reckoning and the distributing path been fulfilled.

"(4) No Money may be lent with usury for purpose of trade, for this is ungodly and usurious, also harmful and noxious to the Commonweal, without weighing of gain and of loss to take or to give monies or usury.

"(5) No sort of Ware may be brought into one hand.

"(6) Dispersed Companies may not join themselves together, on pain of losing all their goods.

"(7) No Merchant may buy at one buying more than 100 hundred-weight of Pepper, 100 hundredweight of Ginger, and of no manner of Spice which hath the name, more than 50 hundred-weight; also after such buying he may not buy or trade any more of the same Ware for the fourth part of a year.

Inasrnuch as especial nimbleness is used by the great Companies, the which have their knowledge in many lands, when the Wares spoil or when they come into greater worth, so as they make foreign Merchants buy up frorn others that have such Wares and bring the same into their hands before the others do know of such loss. Therefrom there followeth a great dearness of the Ware. For the other part the punishment may be best set in such wise that should such a harmful sale be disclosed Within four weeks from the making thereof, the buyer shall be bound thereunto that he surrender his Ware again to the seller for the one half that was paid therefor; the other half part of the price falleth to the Authority.

"(9) On pain of loss of the Goods, as hath been determined in Köln, the seller rnay not make condition that the buyer shall not dare to give away the Wares for a lesser price.

"(10) In order that foreign nations may not be healed and bettered the while German land is oppressed and despoiled, it is commanded that this ordinance shall bind all foreigners born without who have their Storehouse within the Empire; so that a foreigner, whether a Frenchman or whatsoever he may be, that tradeth in the Holy Empire and is encompassed by this ordinance, shall and must suffer all penalties even as other Merchants born in this country, that do transgress. This shall also bind all Principalities, Lordships and Cities, even though they be free, to the intent that it shall be held equally for all men, and that none shall therein be spared.

"(11) Through the voyaging of German Merchants to Portugal there ariseth great evil, in that in Lisabon, because of the shipping from Portugal to the Indies with Spices and other matters, there be great Storehouses and very bold buying and selling, such as can in no wise else exist in one place, and therefore in that place ariseth the great due and enhancement of every manner of Spice and Ware which are borne away from thence, the same also with the pennyworths which they use up even in Portugal, and may not succeed with till they be once more shipped from the Indies to that city. To this end must every Ware that cometh from Portugal be ventured on the sea by Germans and be bound upon the Wheel of Fortune; and the voyage to Portugal is well-nigh more fearsome and dangerous than is that to the Indies. In few years on this same sea hath the worth of fifteen hundreds of thousands of Gulden been drowned and perished; and yet nevertheless are the Merchant folk, who have inherited but little, become so unspeakably rich. Therefore shall all shipping to Portugal be forbidden; the Portuguese shall themselves take in hand the venture and their Wares, and those that they may not keep they shall bring to Germany; for if one cloth not thus pursue them, they must perforce sell at a lesser price. Others do affirm, indeed, that if the Portuguese do bring their Wares to Antorff (Antwerp), then would the great Companies find there also means to buy up the Wares; and the King of Portugal inay be moved to get the Ware to Danzig or Egen Merten (Aigues Mortes) in France, so that the Germans must fetch them thence. But others would show, forsooth, that because of his receiving of the metals he cannot spare Germany, and without them he can do no trade to the Indies; one must therefore but hinder his receiving of the metals, and thus shall one compel him not to trade to France.

"(12) There shall be a fixing of the price of some Wares, to the end that not merely is it ordered for the common hucksters and Merchant folk, but also for them that buy these Wares for their own use and pleasure. It is to fear that also the scattered Companies do agree together secretly to sell over the price; moreover, hath the King of Portugal the Spices in his power alone, and since that time can he set the prices as he will, because for no manner of dearness will they rest unsold among the Germans. Moreover, it hath been related from Refel and Lubeck that the King of Denmark and the Fuggers stand in trade, the one with the other, that all Merchants' goods that have hitherto come from Muscoy (Moscow) into the German trading cities shall further come to Denmark, and into the might of the King thereof and of the Fuggers, to the end that they rnay enhance the same at their pleasure. Thus far have men not punished such things with just pains, but have wittingly borne with them. Such can alone be made

150

riddance of by a forbidding, that they and the Wares may not be sold in Gerinany higher than for a price determined. *The Regiment (Imperial governing Body,) shall tax each ware by the hundredweight to a fixed sum.* As measure shall the customary middle prices serve as they have been wont to be before the Wares have come into the power of the King of Portugal and of the great, hurtful, forbidden Companies. But question may be made: what though the Wares should miscarry? Then shall the Merchant folk recover themselves in them that do succeed. But what if there be lack of those Wares ? The foreigners can far less spare our money than we their Wares; therefore is there in the Empire no long enduring, hurtful lack to be feared; *unless it should he that one should esteem the not giving out in vain of money for a lack.* By such ordinance shall the danger of the overweening raising of prices be best hindered. In the matter of the dues the remoteness of the places can be made consideration of, also the diversncss of the measures and the weights; thus will the Pepper in the storehouse in Frankfort be taxed at one Kreutzer the pound and even so in Nürnberg. The due shall begin one half year after the determination thereof by the Imperial Estates.

"Fuither, it shall not be that the Merchants shall lend money to the poor folk upon pledge of the seed that standeth in the field, or upon the grapes of the vine-stems and other fruits, whereby these poor, needy people have that taken from them that they do hardy earn.

"Thereupon shall follow penalties for all transgressors as for careless authorities; the leave that each may indite before the Fiscal; the determination that all confiscated goods wherewith transgressions have been committed shall fall, the half to the Imperial Fiscus, the half to the [local] authority. The Fiscal shall also proceed against the

Companies which have enriched themselves openly against right and justice; if this do befal, it shall not alone feed the Fiscus but shall also warn others to guard themselves from such evil hurtfulness. The ordinance concerning the sale, etc., shall be put in work two months after it bath been proclaimed.

"It be also considered that the safe conduct of the highways is beneficial to the Merchants' calling, so that all traders may traffic and travel more safely on the highways of the Holy Empire than bath befallen for long time past.

"It chanceth that certain Merchants deceitfully in the seeming of trust and faith do take the Goods of other men by making bankruptcy, which is like unto a theft, and he who doth of purpose strive after another man's Money and Goods shall be punished hardly.

"In fine, there be Imperial Measures and Weights needed; for the falsifying of Cloths and Wares it behoveth a grievous treatment, and the Estates are warned to beware of cunning and greedy and suborned procurations, whereby this ordinance may be brought to nought by the Companies." (N.B. — Hereby is meant according to a notice from another hand: "by a bribing of the authorities so that by their *favor* and *patrocinium* the pains of this ordinance may be escaped".)

I have given the above document at length, as it is curious and instructive, for more than one reason. In the first place, it indicates the Imperial German centralisation in several ways attempted during the reigns of Maximilian and Charles V., on the lines of the recent centralising administrations of England, France and Spain. It also shows us Germany commanding the bullion of Europe to a great extent. This was, of course, in consequence of the wealth of the trading cities, especially of the Hanse and

Bavarian towns. The importance of the spice trade is also strikingly illustrated; and on this point the document may well give rise to various reflections as to the character of late medieval cookery. Last, but not least, we see the hostility of the proud feudal prince or baron and his legal assessor to the *Parvenu* and *Nouvcau riche*, then for the first time appearing on the scene.

Appendix B

Ten closely printed folio pages of Sebastian Franck's *Chronica* (published in 1531) are taken up with a seemingly exhaustive narrative of the incident referred to in the text; albeit Franke himself tells us that it only represents a small portion — the "kernel," as he expresses it — of what he had prepared, and indeed actually written, on the subject, the bulk of which, however, the exigencies of space compelled him to suppress.

"In the year 1509," says Franck, "the two Orders of the 'Preachers' (Dominicans) and 'Barefooted Friars' (Franciscans) did wax hot against one another concerning the conception of Mary. The 'Barefooted' did hold that she was pure from all original sin and spotless; the 'Preachers,' that she was conceived in original sin even as other children of men. Now there was, much debate thereon, and at Heidelberg was there a disputation .... In the end came it to pass that the 'Preachers' (Dominicans) did devise to further their matter and opinion with false signs and wonders."

A certain Dominican preacher, Wigandus by name, who had written a book against the Immaculate Conception, advised resort to trickery. The suggestion was adopted in a full Chapter of the Order held at Wimpfen in 1506. Nürnberg and Frankfort were thought of as suitable places, but on consideration were rejected on the ground that the townsfolk of these two commercial centres were too sharp-witted. Eventually, Bern was decided upon. Accordingly, four Dominicans, the Prior, the sub-Prior, the chief preacher and another monk, connected with a foundation possessed by the Order at that place, were instructed to set about the business. They got hold of a young journeyman tailor, who

155

applied to be received into the Order, and whom they admitted with apparent reluctance on payment of fifty-three gulden, besides the gift of some damascene and silk. As soon as they had him well in hand, they began to test his credulity by playing practical jokes on him at night — by throwing things into his cell, making mysterious noises and the like, pretending that it was the work of a spirit. At last the Prior came one night enveloped in a white linen sheet, and with horrible noises and gestures seized the trembling novice as he lay in his bed. The latter, of course, screamed and invoked the Mother of God. Upon this, the ghost adjured him, alleging that he and his colleagues could render him inestimable aid if they would but scourge themselves for eight days in succession, and read eight masses in the chapel of St. John. With this the spectre left him.

The youth next day told everything in an agony of fear. The chief preacher of the Order, Dr. Steffan, improved the occasion by an harangue against the Franciscans, declaring that no distressed spirit ever held parley with such unmitigated scoundrels as they were, or sought the aid of such notorious evil-livers. Finally, he succeeded in stirring up a strong feeling in the town against the rival Order.

The four conspiring monks having tested the silly youth, and finding him staunch in his belief, exhorted him to be of good courage the following night, the Prior having purified his cell with holy water and guarded it with relics. But the spirit came again; and on being interrogated, in accordance with instructions given to the novice, the ghost declared itself the soul of a former Prior of the monastery, who had been deposed for loose living, had left the cloister in lay attire, had become involved in a "bad business," and had been stabbed to death in a brawl unshrived. The spirit went on to extol the Dominican Order at the expense of the Franciscans, who would shortly, it predicted, be the ruin of the town of Bern.

Visions of a similar character occurred on the following nights. The preacher, Dr. Steffan, entrusted the novice with a letter containing leading questions favourable to the Order which he was to endeavour to get delivered to the Mother of God, and return with the answers affixed. The letter was subsequently found deposited miraculously in the pyx, and sprinkled with blood said to be of Christ, and sealed with the wine. The letter was the following day laid with great pomp on the high altar. The next night one of the four monks appeared to the novice, dressed as the Virgin, with exuberant praises of the Order, and with instructions to implore the Holy Man, Pope Julius I1., to institute a festival in honour of the "spotted conception" of the Virgin, promising at the same time to convey to him a cross with three spots of the blood of her Son upon it, as a testimony of the truth of her having been born in original sin. She gave him a cloth soaked in blood from the wound in the side, and other relics. She further pierced the guileless youth's hand with a pin, and made him call out, comforting him with the assurance that the wound would reopen afresh twice a year — on Good Friday and Corpus Christi Day. Thereupon the monk-Virgin disappeared.

All things had gone successfully up to this time, and the four monks now decided to officially announce the novice as an inspired person. To this end they succeeded "by magical practices," says Franck — in preparing a water which deprived the new Brother of his senses, and another water which, while in this state, they rubbed into his hands and feet, producing wounds. With a third water they caused him to wake up — delighted to see the new miracles worked upon him. They then gave him a special room to himself, where the "faithful laity" might see him but no one was allowed to speak to him, for fear of his compromising the Order.

Meanwhile these things began to be noised abroad and were eagerly discussed, everybody wishing to get a sight of the new god. At length the long-suffering novice, on another visitation, recognised the voice of the Prior in the sham Virgin, and drawing a knife, stabbed him in the right hip, after which the Prior, seizing a dish from the wall, flung it at the novice and decamped. No blandishments or warnings from the sub-Prior or other monks would induce the now disillusioned novice to allow himself to be made a fool of any longer. Finding this side of the business at an end, they next entreated him with promises not to ruin himself and them, but to throw in his lot with them and consent to hoodwink the people. He, at length, agreed with some reluctance. Then they instructed him in the rôle he was to play. He was to represent an image of the Virgin in the Lady Chapel, whilst Dr. Steffan was to be concealed behind a curtain, and, speaking through a tube, to personify her "Divine Son". The "Son" asked the "Mother" why she wept. The "Mother" answered that she wept because her commands had not been carried out fully as yet. In the meantime some old women, who had been admitted into the chapel, rushed away spreading the report everywhere that the image of the Virgin had wept and spoken. A large concourse assembled in the chapel, amongst them being the four monks, who affected great astonishment. Presently the Bürgermeister with three other high civic functionaries arrived, and demanded of the prior and monks what was the meaning of the great commotion. The Prior replied that the Virgin had wept for the approaching ruin of the whole town of Bern, because it was receiving a pension from the French king, and because it tolerated in its midst the Franciscans with their wicked heresy of the Immaculate Conception, whereby they imputed to her an honour that did not belong to her and which she repudiated. The elders of the city thought it a remarkable occurrence, and looked grave.

The monks now thought to give the novice, the alleged intermediary of so many divine messages, a poisoned sacrament in the presence of the people, so that he might die suddenly, and that they might thus gain two points — be rid of a dangerous witness, and supply their Order with a saint, whom Christ had taken to Himself during; the reception of the Holy Elements. But our novice declined the wafer with the red spots, which was offered him, and which was alleged to be sprinkled with the

158

blood of Christ; and insisted on partaking of a less miraculous-looking one. Nevertheless, the monks did not give up their project, for the novice overheard the next night a secret conclave of the four as to the best way of getting rid of him, whether they should starve him, drown him, strangle him, run him through the body, or choke him. He now began to feel seriously anxious, snore especially as he found his rations diminishing daily. Accordingly, one day he crept out of his cell and followed one of the four monks into the refectory, where he saw them eating capons and drinking wines with girls, who, to his intense disgust, he observed wore dresses made of the very damascene and silk he had contributed to the monastery on his initiation. His presence was detected, and Dr. Steffan tried to pass the girls off as sisters of his own. The monks thought, notwithstanding, that it was high time "to leave their damnable faces and begin". So they gave the novice cabbage stewed in a solution of crushed spiders, but this did him no harm. They then tried it on a cat, which died. The Prior next brought him a poisoned soup, which he did not eat but threw away. Five young wolves kept in the monastery thereupon ate it and died. Then they tried the sacrament trick again, forcing it into his mouth, but he threw it up on to a footstool, which the worthy Sebastian assures us immediately began to sweat blood. This alarmed the conspirators, and they changed their tactics, chaining the youth up, fettling him in various parts of the body with hot irons, until he swore a solemn oath not to divulge anything. At last, says Sebastian, the matter "became too heavy for the Brother," and he resolved to escape at once. He succeeded in doing so by cunning and stealth, and rushing into the town he informed everybody he met of all that had happened. The authorities, however, were unwilling to lay violent hands on a spiritual Order.

The monks, on their side, lost no time in sending their preacher and the sub-Prior to Rome, in order to get the Pope's attestation of their story. They were supported by the whole influence of the Dominican Order throughout Central Europe.

The Rath of Bern then also sent to Rome to demand an impartial judge for the matter, and Pope Julius II. nominated a commission consisting of three priests and a Dominican Provincial. The latter, being seen by one of the bishops admonishing Dr. Steffan how to act, was removed from the court, and died at Constance from vexation. The four monks were then placed on the rack, and revealed everything. The boor novice was also given a few turns on the rack, in order to make sure that he had told all he knew. He rehearsed everything including the story of the girls.

It came out in the course of the trial that Jews' blood, nineteen hairs from the black eyebrow of a Jew child, and other ingredients, which our modest Sebastian informs us "it were not seemly to tell of," went to constitute the magical decoction that the monks had used in order to make the novice subservient to them. It was found also that the sub-Prior had stolen five hundred golden from the monastic chest, and that the other monks had taken the precious stones from the image of the Virgin and disposed of them, also that the Prior had boasted that he could work his will with any woman on whom he laid his hand.

The bishops wanted to transfer the matter to Rome, but the lay authorities would not hear of this, and insisted on the court being reinforced by eight honourable councillors of the city. In the end the ecclesiastics consented to reconstitute the court in this form. The result was a sentence of degradation and burning alive on all four monks. The execution was carried out in the presence of a large concourse of people in the great market-place of the city of Bern, on the 31st of May, 1509.

As intimated in the body of this work, the foregoing affair caused a profound impression over a wide area, affecting as it did the honour and integrity of so powerful an Order as that of the "Preachers" or Dominicans, and it made the city and canton of Bern an easy prey to the reforming' tendencies which came in vogue a few years later.

The following is another illustration of the ready credulity

160

of a mediaeval populace and the excessive excitability of the public mind in the earlier years of the sixteenth century. To quote, this time literally, from another portion of Sebastian Franck's *Chronica*:

"Anno 1516, Dr. Balthasar Hubmeyer [at this time Hubmeyer was still a Catholic] did preach with vehemence against the Jews at Regensburg, showing how great an evil doth arise to the whole German nation, not alone from their faith, but also from their usury, and how unspeakable a tribute their usury doth bear away withal. Then was there a Council held that they should pray the Emperor to the end that Jews might be driven forth. Therefore did they the people break their synagogue in pieces, also many of their houses, and did build in the place thereof a Temple in honour of Mary, to which they gave the name of The Fair Mary. This did some visit privily, and told that from that hour was their prayer fulfilled. So soon, therefore, as the matter became noised abroad, even then was there a running from all parts thither, as though the people were bewitched, of wife, of child, of gentlemen, some spiritual, some worldly, they coming so long a way, it might be having eaten nothing. Certain children who knew not the road did come from afar with a piece of bread, and the people came with so manifold an armoury, even such as it chanced that each had, the while he was at his work, the one with a milking-pail, the other with a hay-fork. Some there were that had scarce aught on in the greatest cold, wherewithal to cover them in barest need. Some there were that did run many miles without speaking, as they might be half-possessed or witless; some did come barefoot with rakes, axes and sickles; these had fled from the fields and forsaken their lords; some caméd in a shirt they had by chance laid hands on as they arose from their bed; some did come at midnight; some there were that ran day and night; and there was in all such a running from all lands that, in the space of but one day, many thousands of men had come in.

"One there was that saw miracles from so much and so divers silver, gold, wax, pictures and jewels that were brought thither. There were daily so many masses read that one priest could scarce but meet the other, as he departed from the altar. When one did read the Communion (Commun], the other even then did kneel before the altar with his Confiteor. These things came to pass daily till well-nigh beyond noon, and although many altars were set up both within and without the Temple, yet nevertheless could not one priest but encounter the other.

"The learned did sing many Carmina in praise of Fair Mary, and many and divers offices were devised of signs, of pipes and of organs. Much sick folk did they lead and bear thither, and also, as some do believe, dead men whom they brought home again restored and living. There befel also many great signs and wonders, the which it would not be fitting to tell of, and whereof all especial cheat was rumoured, in that what any brought thither, did he but vow himself with his offering, straightway was he healed, not alone from his sicknesses, but the living did receive also their dead again, the blind saw, the halt ran, did leave their crutches in the Temple, and walked upright from thence. Some ran thither from the war; yea, wives from their husbands, children from the obedience and will of their fathers would thither, saying that they might not remain away, and that they had no rest day nor night.

"Some as they entered into the Temple and beheld the image straightway fell down as though the thunder had smote them. As the mad rabble beheld how such did fall, they bethought them that it were the power of God, and that each must needs fall in this place. Thus there came to

162

pass such a falling (such as was a foolishness and unrestrained and of the devil's likeness) that well-nigh each that came to these places did fall, and many from the rabble, who did not fall, believed themselves to be unholy and did enforce themselves straightway to fall, till the Council [Rath] was moved, as they say, to forbid such, and then did the signs and fallings cease.

"It is wondrous to relate with what strange Instruments the people caméd thither; as one was seized in the midst of his labour, lie took not the time to lay aside that which he held in his hand but bore it with him, and each ran unshrived away, being driven by his own spirit. But whether the great Holy Spirit did move to such ill-considered tumult against obedience, did drive the mother from the child, the wife from the husband, the servant and the child contrary to the obedience to be rendered to the master and the father, I will leave to others to determine. Many do even believe as I do, that it cannot be the work of God inasmuch as it is contrary to His word, work, manner, nature and the interpretation of the Scriptures.

"Now this running toward hath held a goodly season, as it may be six or eight years, but hath now ceased, albeit not wholly."

I have reproduced as literally as possible from Franck's own language, not (as will have been noticed) omitting or toning down the repetitions and incoherences of style.

Appendix C

The celebrated family of Fugger of Augsburg migrated to that city about the year 1370 from a village near Schwabmünchen. What their precise status was in their original home is not very clear; but they would seem to have been above the rank of ordinary peasants, and it is just possible that they may have been *Freier* or freeholders of land without nobility. At all events, they are said to have cultivated flax and hemp somewhat extensively. The two brothers, Ulrich and Johannes Fugger, on arriving in Augsburg, devoted themselves to weaving of wool and linen, and became master-wearers, possessing several looms. Through marriage they soon acquired the citizenship, and the family continued to rise and flourish during the fifteenth century. Some time before 1450, a Fugger became Grand Master of the Weavers' Guild, and towards the close of that century Ulrich Fugger was one of the first to take advantage of the rising world-market and of the dislocated feudal conditions of the time. In 1473, he had to settle the financial affairs of Maximilian, who wished to lend money to Charles the Bold. For his services on this occasion he and his brothers were ennobled, and received "lily" as their armorial device. Ulrich was also a patron of Albrecht Dürer, and it was through him that Dürer's pictures were sent into Italy.

Ulrich Fugger bought from Pope Alexaner VI. the patronage of a canonry near St. Moritz for a thousand ducats. In 1494 he and his brother inaugurated the trade syndicates spoken of in the preceding pages by a company for trading in spices. It is referred to in the Reichstag rescript given in Appendix A. Ulrich died in 1510, leaving seven daughters and three sons; his brother had already died in 1506. They had bought up all the houses on the Weinmarkt, and converted them into a palace, in which they lived conjointly.

Jacob Fugger, a younger son of Ulrich, raised the family

to the zenith of its opulence and magnificence. Originally brought up for the Church, he became a canon; but later, on the wish of his father, he renounced the tonsure and devoted himself to commerce. He first went to reside in Venice, in order to get mercantile training in the family warehouse which the Fuggers had established in that city. Venice was then, and for long afterwards, a kind of training school for the merchants of the South German cities. Jacob also made further journeys to the principal commercial towns of Europe, the result of his studies and travels being the expansion of his family business to a degree previously unheard of in the annals of medieval trading. To such a point did he carry his success that soon his wool, silk and spinning business generally, became a mere subordinate matter with him, his chief occupations being mining and banking. Jacob Fugger was, in fact, the first great European capitalist, the Rothschild and Vanderbilt of his day.

In Spain, in the Tyrol, in Hungary and in Carinthia, he bought up lands rich in ore from derelict and impecunious nobles, and succeeded in opening up valuable silver, copper and lead mines. Paracelsus mentions having visited the Fugger mines at Schwatz in the Tyrol in connection with his alchemistic studies. The new route to India afforded by the discovery of the Cape Passage gave Fugger the opportunity of showing his ability to seize a timely advantage from changing conditions. In 1505, lie joined with the two other large commercial houses, those of Welser and Hochstetten, in an undertaking for shipping three cargoes of Indian wares. This class of goods had hitherto come over land by way of the Levant and Venice; but now, for the first time, they were shipped direct from the East Indies by the new Cape route.

The previous year, 1504, Jacob and his brothers had been ennobled by the Emperor Maximilian, Jacob himself being made Imperial Councillor. Leo X. further constituted him Count Palatine and *Eques Aureatus*. In 1509, Jacob advanced Maximilian as much as 170,000 ducats as a subsidy towards the cost of the Italian War. Subsequently, on the election of Charles V. to the Imperial dignity, he contributed 300,000 ducats to the expenses involved. On one occasion, when he entertained Charles V. as a guest in his palace on the Weinmarkt in Augsburg, he burnt the overdue "acceptances" of the Emperor on a large fire of cinnamon, at that time one of the most costly spices.

The Fuggers acquired in the shape of fallen-in mortgages several feudal territories, comprising numerous villages. In fact, by their financial operations alone, apart from their enormous mercantile transactions, the family amassed an immense fortune. Jacob enlarged the great Fugger palace already referred to, and added a sumptuous choir to the Augsburg church of St. Anna. He also founded the "Fuggerei," an entire quarter of Augsburg still extant, to be used as almshouses for poor citizens. He died in 1525, leaving as his heirs his two nephews Raimond and Anton.

Residing together in the Fugger palace, they still further added to the renown of their family by their patronage of the new learning and the fine arts. They tool: a distinguished place as patricians in the Rath of their native city, and they were raised by Charles V. into the ranks of the higher nobility as hereditary counts of the Empire, being also granted lands with hereditary jurisdiction. By their operations in finance, they still further increased the territorial acquisitions of their family. All contemporary writers descant on the pomp and munificence of the Fugger establishment. The family continued to flourish up to the Thirty Years' War, in which they played a considerable part on the Imperial Catholic side. The history of the Fuggers, of their enrichment by gigantic mercantile operations on the basis of the world-market, of the new developments they gave to the time-old practice of money lending, and of the fresh energy and improved methods employed in their mining enterprises, affords a typical instance of the birth and rapid growth of the new constructive principle of capitalism — a birth and growth taking place *pari passu* with the destructive processes of the disintegration of Feudalism.